TREE TREK

TREE TREK

*A Daughter's Walk
Through Grief*

A Memoir

*Written and Illustrated
by Stephanie Mirocha*

Holy Cow! Press
Duluth, Minnesota
2025

Text and all illustrations, copyright © 2025 by Stephanie Mirocha. All rights reserved. No part of this book may be reproduced without permission of the Author and Publisher.

Cover art and design by Stephanie Mirocha.
Interior design by Anton Khodakovsky.

Author photograph and all interior photographs by Stephanie Mirocha, unless otherwise noted on page 121.

Printed and bound in the United States.
First printing, Spring, 2025

10 9 8 7 6 5 4 3 2 1

Library of Congress Cataloging Number: 2024027263
ISBN 978-1666406931 (paperback)
ISBN 978-1666406948 (eBook)

Holy Cow! Press projects are funded in part by grant awards from the Ben and Jeanne Overman Charitable Trust, the Elmer L. and Eleanor J. Andersen Foundation, The Lenfestey Family Foundation, The Woessner Freeman Family Foundation, and by gifts from generous individual donors. We are grateful to Springboard for the Arts for their support as our fiscal sponsor.

Holy Cow! Press books are distributed to the trade by Consortium Book Sales & Distribution, c/o Ingram Publisher Services, Inc., 210 American Drive, Jackson, TN 38301.

For inquiries, please write to: *Holy Cow! Press*, Post Office Box 3170, Mount Royal Station, Duluth, MN 55803.

Visit *www.holycowpress.org*

*To true friends, including trees,
and especially Erling*

Table of Contents
List of Illustrations

Introduction		1
Cotyledons of an American Basswood (Tilia americana)		
Chapter 1.	Basswood (Genus *Tilia*). Family Connections	7
	American Basswood (Tilia americana)	
Chapter 2.	Spruce (Genus *Picea*). Transformation	17
	White Spruce (Picea glauca)	
Chapter 3.	Maple (Genus *Acer*). Separation and Hanging On	27
	Red Maple (Acer rubrum)	
Chapter 4.	Oak (Genus *Quercus*). Leaving and Letting Go	35
	Bur Oak (Quercus macrocarpa)	
Chapter 5.	Northern White Cedar (Genus *Thuja*). Healing Words and Gentle Touch	39
	Northern White Cedar (Thuja occidentalis)	
Chapter 6.	Douglas-fir (Genus *Pseudotsuga*). Finding a New Fit	47
	Douglas-fir (Pseudotsuga menziesii)	
Chapter 7.	Pine (Genus *Pinus*). Being Present with Grief	55
	Eastern White Pine (Pinus strobus)	
Chapter 8.	Pea (Family Fabaceae). Feeding the Soil	63
	Black Locust (Robinia pseudoacacia)	
Chapter 9.	Poplar (Genus *Populus*). Finding Meaning in Names	73
	White Poplar (Populus alba)	
Chapter 10.	Ginkgo (Genus *Ginkgo*). Millennia of Life Renewing	83
	Ginkgo (Ginkgo biloba)	
Chapter 11.	Hackberry (Genus *Celtis*). Galaxies Crossing	93
	Common Hackberry (Celtis occidentalis)	
Chapter 12.	Seed-bearing Plants (Spermatophytes). Listening	103
	A Forest Ecosystem of Spermatophytes	
Acknowledgments		113
Author's Note		115
Bibliography		117
Our Tree Treks		121
About the Author and Artist		123

Introduction

ONE WEEK BEFORE MY DAD DIED, HE LOST HIS ABILITY TO SPEAK. AT FIRST, HE stopped articulating words, which progressed into a state of silent communication. He also lost fine motor skills in his hands for holding a pen or typing. He was lucky. His disease gave him no pain, only weakness as his body shut down. A few days before he died, the most he could do was to accept help to the bathroom and back to bed. One evening after returning to bed, he attempted to relay something on his mind. Before he lay down, he made a gesture with forefinger across palm, pantomiming the act of writing. My sister, Julie, was with me helping him, but my dad looked at me as he did this.

"What is it, Dad? Do you need something?" I asked.

He shook his head no, closed his eyes for a bit, then made the same sign again. Though I knew his hands were too weak for writing, I had no recourse but to ask anyway,

"Do you want pencil and paper?"

He shook his head again. I could see he was tiring and that this was taking a lot of effort, but clearly there was something he wanted to say. I felt at a loss, helpless to get him what he wanted. The inability to understand was frustrating for me, a feeling that probably went both ways.

"Dad," I said, "I'm sorry. I just don't understand."

He gave a little shrug of defeat. We left him tucked beneath his down comforter in the darkness and took ourselves off to bed after a tiring day of caregiving.

The next morning, I woke with a sudden understanding of what my dad had been trying to say and feeling very eager for a chance to confirm it. That moment arrived soon enough when we returned from the bathroom and he sat on the side of the bed again, resting. With my hand in his view, I moved my forefinger across my palm and said, "Dad, I think I finally figured out what you meant last night."

He looked up, listening.

"You were encouraging me to keep writing. Is that it?"

He nodded enthusiastically and softly clapped his hands. To receive this loving affirmation filled me with a radiant sensation of being seen, heard, and supported.

This book is the story of losing my father, that pillar in my life, and of trees, the silent partners who stood by me along the way. My dad and I shared a deep love of nature that began early with family camping trips and later expanded as the two of us enjoyed many one-on-one adventures together as I grew into adulthood. In middle school there was a hike, referenced often between us later, through unexpectedly dense clouds of mosquitoes forcing us to improvise on the spot by stuffing fern fronds under our hats in a desperate attempt to ward them off. We skied many times through remote wilderness and groomed courses alike. We camped in a favorite primitive area he discovered along a creek that had no trail in. He surprised me one day in grade school by appearing during library hour, giving the teacher some excuse to take me out of class for the day. He was excited to share with me a new state forest he had just found.

My dad's field of work was in plant pathology, the study of plant diseases arising from the microorganisms (the fungi, bacteria, viruses, and nematodes) that cause them. In his retirement, he began a new pursuit: learning to identify trees in our nearby city park along with some of their diseases, then taking this knowledge and sharing it with the community. As he became more involved with park activities, my dad innovated educational walks through trees in an event he named Como Park Tree Trek. During that time and onward he liked to quote from *The Lorax* by Dr. Suess, saying he was "speaking for the trees." Now that he is no longer here, I continue to speak for the trees in the same way, bringing to my work in the park my own version of passion and enthusiasm. This is how I carry on his legacy. This story could have happened in any community with a diversity of trees, any city park or natural area, and in any city where a special guy with a passion for science, trees, and nature lived. It just happened to take place in Como Regional Park, "my" beloved park, the 450 acre city park in St. Paul, Minnesota located across the street from my childhood home, the house in which my mom still lives.

In this book, each chapter title names a tree followed by its genus or family name (grouping species as relatives). I did not plan the trees that head the chapters; they just came along in the process of writing, like characters in a novel who appear in the imagination and seem just right. As characters, trees don't say very much, at least not in the way we are accustomed to hearing, but they were right there beside me as I wrote during the several weeks-long pouring out of a rainstorm of feelings and ideas formed from my grief. Trees provided the paper for this explosion of words, including the pages you now hold.

In my scientific study of trees, I have learned the particular traits and idiosyncrasies of each species which, in a nonscientific way, imbues them with personality. As my dad used to say about any species, "That's their nature, just the way (fill in the blank) are." These traits can reflect our own inner natures and make connections to our own lives. A swamp white oak in winter holding onto its leaves may strike some people as stubborn, others as steadfastly persevering, still others as merely decorative, or it might make a connection to some memory from long ago. Depending on what experiences we bring to the situation, we will be drawn to one or more favorite trees that somehow speak to us. They reflect what we need, like healing from grief, as we focus both within ourselves and beyond ourselves at the same time. In this way, trees bring us home.

Let's fill in my dad's blank with "juniper." Imagine a juniper coming into view as we walk through the forest. Juniper stands there pure, unmasked, with no agenda at all. Something makes us stop and admire her, feeling her truth flow through us. What does juniper give us? Different things for different people. She is just benignly there, presenting her dark blue "berries" amidst her prickly fronds, always extending an invitation to rest beneath for a while and contemplate…what?

That is for you to find out!

There are many paths to take through grief. Nature offers one way to help move through this powerful emotion and find our way forward, but each path is different and deeply personal. As you walk with me on my grief trek through the trees in these pages, my hope is to open one possible doorway for you to process your own suffering. I have found that spending time in nature offers a trail leading directly into the heart, and, at the very least, to a sense of calm. This is doable for everyone because we are part of nature. The calmness we find beyond ourselves reflects the meditative truth and beauty of our own inner wisdom shining from within. One key moment is all it takes to start things in motion.

For me, that key moment happened when I least expected it one day after crossing Como Park's pedestrian bridge on a break from caregiving during the last few weeks of my dad's life. The family had been slowly coalescing into making plans to help as the seriousness of his health condition became apparent. Of my five siblings, only one, Mary, lived in the metro area; the rest ranged from Anne in southeastern Wisconsin near Madison, Paul in Arizona, Andrew in Washington, and Julie out in California.

My husband, Erling, and I live two and a half hours north of St. Paul. We both make our living from the arts. Over the last several years, we intentionally booked art shows in the metro area to stay with my parents and help out however we could ever since my mom's first diagnosis of dementia a few years earlier. So, we were on hand when the first dire signs of my dad's deteriorating condition appeared. One morning about a month before he died, my dad lacked the strength to return upstairs after he came down for breakfast and coffee. Upon seeing how weak he was, how the only way he could return upstairs was by pushing himself backwards up the steps one at a time, Erling and I immediately decided to cancel our show for which we had been about to head out the door and shift our focus completely onto my dad.

From there, for me it was endless coordinating with doctors, appointment ferrying, meds, and communication with siblings. Erling headed back home off and on during these weeks as we continued to cancel shows, but this was our choice. Sometimes the coffee was too hot—other times too cold. There was a lot of running up and down the stairs. It was good to have other help slowly arriving for this basic care that evolved into total care. Meanwhile, my mom, Donna, required another person (or more) assigned the task of keeping her away from my dad. Her dementia brought out the worst qualities of her anxiety, and she needed monitoring because of severe short-term memory loss. The household had always been her domain, and her inability to let go amounted to constant interfering. Just seeing her enter his room once again would send my dad's blood pressure sky high.

"Get her out of here," he'd yell.

And she did require a lot of attention. I recall one ironic moment that exemplifies those last weeks. My dad was in bed in the guest room, going about the business of dying without too much fuss, separated by a wall from their shared bedroom where my mom, also in bed but with a mild condition, kept calling out, "My ear hurts!" Unintentionally of course, she pestered him constantly, and he really couldn't take it anymore, which made for a very difficult household situation. Keeping her away from him wasn't easy, as Erling can attest to. He was kicked in the legs on multiple occasions, whether he was trying to block her way upstairs to my dad or hold her back when she raced out the front door in an attempt to stop my dad and I from driving away to a medical appointment without her. A block away I would often pull over for a minute just to recover. Since I was there for most of that time, I took on a coordinating role, keeping communication going between everyone to avoid chaos as my dad grew weaker and weaker.

Breaks were necessary, and as my siblings began to arrive and come on board this was clear to everyone. My key moment, as I was saying, happened on one of those escapes from the house on a break that typically consisted of a hike through the park. As I finished crossing the pedestrian bridge that day on my way back, instead of looking straight ahead at the Lily Pond as I usually did, for some reason my head turned to the left and my gaze fell directly on an Ohio buckeye tree. On its trunk was one of my dad's tree ID signs shining starkly as if looking at me, drawing my attention to it like an arrow. It was the first time I had ever noticed one of his tree signs I'd heard about from vague references slipped into conversations over the last several years. I'd only been aware of these peripherally. It's possible I had seen them and not taken in their meaning fully or had seen them but just not given them a second thought. This time, though, the sight moved from my peripheral awareness right into center focus—boom!—instantly connecting me to my dad. In that moment, something rang true within, pealing like a small bell ringing from my heart. I veered over to the buckeye, wanting to find out more about these trees with signs.

How many were there in the park? Where were all the other ones located? I felt as if I were moving through a newly formed extra dimension—no going back—that in a millisecond had united my love for trees with my love for my dad, bringing it all together. The way forward opened. Speaking for the trees lay ahead for me, but I had no idea of that then. I simply stood beneath the buckeye tree clinging to that feeling of closeness with my dad, holding on, ready to follow wherever this new path would lead because I knew it would take me somewhere I needed to go.

A seed that is ready to germinate requires only the right conditions in which to split open and release its first leaf (or leaves) occurring singly, in a pair, or in a whorl of several depending on the species. Commonly called the seed leaf, or more intriguingly in Latin and botany known as the cotyledon (pronounced "ka-tuh-LEE-dun"), these primary leaves look nothing like the true leaves still to come and exist solely to nourish and support those on the way. They are actually part of the seed embryo itself, serving to access stored nutrients that help the first true leaves begin supplying their own energy as a growing plant when, at last, the new leaves emerge into the sunlight.

This book is about the cotyledons that exist inside each of us, waiting to begin nourishment in whatever way we need. Given the right conditions to flourish, our cotyledons will release their creative sparks into the world to feed that something that's on the way. We might not know what this thing will look like later—what species of tree we are birthing—but we can feed it, nonetheless.

Like a majestic oak that grows from a small acorn, things take time not only to figure out but also to manifest. Our connection to trees is universal. Who and what are these remarkable life forms we live alongside? There is so much we can learn about them. What, in return, can trees teach us that brings us home to ourselves? Nothing at all, unless we listen, and the way to begin doing that is simple.

We must walk among them.

Chapter 1
Basswood
(Genus *Tilia*)
Family Connections

American basswood (Tilia americana) *is North America's native species, preferring the northern portion of its large range covering the eastern two thirds of Canada into Mexico. Naturally occurring varieties of American basswood fill in the southern portions. White basswood is one, starting in southwestern Pennsylvania following the Appalachians south and appearing as far west as Missouri. Another variety, Virginia basswood, stays south from North Carolina to Florida and west into a few areas of Texas. The southernmost variety, Mexican basswood, overlaps and continues from there. In the mid-1700s, colonists introduced the European counterpart, little-leaf linden* (Tilia cordata), *as an ornamental. Today, this foreign species and its cultivars continue in that decorative role, valued for their pleasing form and smaller growth habit as urban landscape trees cultivated coast to coast.*

BENEATH THE CITY PARK'S AMERICAN BASSWOOD TREE (*TILIA AMERICANA*), otherwise known as American linden, I am crouched. It is a warm, sunny morning in late September, almost two years after my dad's death. The tree I'm under is classified in the genus *Tilia*, the same genus of tree my babcia knew when she was a young girl in Poland. *Babcia* is Polish for grandmother, and she was my dad's mom. *Tilia* goes way back in our family lore ever since Babcia, as an immigrant to the United States at age 19, brought her native language and culture with her, including the healing power of lindens. American basswood has many of the same qualities as the linden species she knew back home in Poland, so it must have been nice for her to find a tree so familiar. Every July, Babcia would gather blossoms from the *Tilia* trees she found growing in her new American neighborhood in Cudahy, Wisconsin. My dad held a very deep love and reverence for his mother, so this tree seems the perfect way to begin my story.

In Polish, the month of July is called *Lipiec*, which derives from the word *lipowy*, meaning "linden" and also from the word *lipa*, which means "lime tree." (In Europe and Great Britain, lindens are also called lime trees.) For a culture to name a month after a tree that blooms during that time reveals the reverence held for this sacred tree in Babcia's native homeland. The flowers she was accustomed to gathering from the European version, little-leaf linden (*Tilia cordata*), bloom a bit later and are a bit more potent than those of its American counterpart, but perhaps only slightly.

Starting in late June and going into July, as if in celebration of summer, *Tilia* trees are laden with thousands of flowers hanging down in glorious white clusters known in botany as cymes. Heat draws out compounds from the flowers into a calming tea, used also for lung congestion. My dad would recall summer days of his mother coming home with a basket of fresh linden flowers, their aromatic fragrance lingering and filling the rooms. She would dry the blossoms in the attic, then make tea from them throughout the year whenever someone in the household came down with a cold. The gentle, supportive words of this quiet woman taking care of her family goes hand in hand with the subtle healing effects that herbs, as medicine, possess.

Basswood flowers grow suspended from light green, leaf-like appendages, called bracts in botany, and are eye-catching enough to make them a good way to identify the tree, for all *Tilia* have bracts. Their light color and slender shape contrast with the broad, dark green leaves, making *Tilia* bracts really stand out. Fertilized flowers form into a nut-like seed that resembles a small berry and ripens late summer into fall. The bracts and their little, round seeds can often hang on into winter, supplying much-needed food for birds and many other forest creatures. In fact, all parts of the basswood tree are edible or used in herbal medicine for humans. In late May, I toss the still small and tender leaves into a refreshing spring salad mix for my family. Bees forsake all else for the intoxicating flowers that are abundantly filled with both nectar and pollen, from which they produce a wonderful honey. This is why the basswood, linden, or lime tree is also known as the bee-tree!

As a seven-year-old, I valued basswood blossoms differently from Babcia. My approach was to gather the dried-up flowers after they fell in the summer and add them to my outdoor play kitchen. In spring, I did the same with the leaf-bud coverings (called scales or perules) that pop off and drop from newly opening buds as the leaves emerge. Moist and tender, perules carpet the ground and lace the edges of puddles for a short time until they dry up and blow away. Every species has their own color, scent, and texture of perules. From my point of view, the huge basswood tree next door offered a nice contrast to our own towering elm tree for my perule collecting. Scraping them up off the driveway and sidewalks, I would separate the different kinds into bowls set out in my backyard play kitchen. The gray, weathered bench that my dad used for sawing wood was my countertop. A rag found on the back porch was draped over a stick held in place on the bench with a brick. One big bowl served as a stew pot to cook up a concoction with my freshly assembled pantry of varied ingredients. All I needed was water from the hose and an old wooden spoon to make me completely absorbed and content.

Perules and their differences, in fact, were what first led me to really notice my neighbor's tree. Their large, heart-shaped leaves as opposed to those on our elm so intrigued me that one day I asked our neighbor what kind of tree it was and made sure to remember the answer.

"Basswood," he said.

"That's a funny name," I replied. "Like a fish made of wood."

He smiled, and, observing the tree, added, "It's getting so big, though, we might have to cut it down."

"I hope you don't do that," I blurted, shocked. I showed him my bowl of perules to convince him of the tree's importance, feeling suddenly helpless at the whims of adults. "See what I do with them?" I asked.

Most likely, each of us has at least one story in which a tree appears. Sharing these is a good way to bring to light the important role these allies play in our lives. Many of us have a tree or special plant that is part of our everyday landscape. They may have become true companions even if we don't realize it.

Over time, we might walk past our tree every day without really noticing. Just like with family or people you see habitually, it's easy to stop clueing into their little changes. In the same way, trees grow so slowly that their subtleties can elude us until something happens to get our attention.

The day this struck home to me was in our house where I live with Erling in Aitkin, a small town in northern Minnesota. One morning, I opened the window blinds to the Scots pine that for decades had peeked up from the other side of the neighbor's garage across the alley. That tree had always been a steadfast part of my getting-up routine, welcoming me to the day, and is something I had almost (not quite) taken for granted. That day, as I lifted the blinds, it struck me how it had grown 25 feet or so in the 30 years I had known it. What a majestic tree it had become right under my nose! How could I have missed this? In that moment, a sense of connectedness with that tree came upon me. I felt so grateful for it simply to be in my life. The next year, unfortunately, my neighbor cut it down, just like our neighbor's basswood beside my childhood home. These departed companions leave holes in the landscape that become cherished memories, just as for any friend or loved one. It's an absence that's not always easy to get used to.

That thought brings me back to the present moment and the reason I'm here at the park's American basswood tree. I'm crouched down beneath it on this late September morning because my fingers have inadvertently dropped a nail in the grass and duff at my feet. Have you ever noticed that when you drop a nail, screw, drill bit, or earring, it immediately disappears into nature? My colleague, Susan Jane, and I search for five minutes and come up empty. I take another nail from my pouch and proceed with our project, affixing tree identification tags to 20 or so exemplar species in the city park. These are trees chosen both for their beauty and location in the general area of where my dad, who initiated this whole endeavor, led his Como Park Tree Treks so many years ago.

Como Park Tree Trek has two versions. One is a scheduled event that happens once or twice a year, a two-hour guided tour connecting people to trees through explanations of their distinguishing characteristics, botany, history, and place in our culture. The other part is a self-guided tree ID tour through the park. Many parks and campuses have this, something a trekker can just do on their own any time of the year. Trees with small, attached signs are always waiting to tell their stories, both with short text and the learning that leads to having confidence in knowing what you are looking at. More observations can take off from that point, convenient and available for further research.

My dad first put his energy into leading Tree Treks. Soon after, he innovated the self-guided aspect, eventually tagging about 18 trees throughout the park. When various factors, including old age, caused my dad to stop leading Tree Treks as an event, that part of the program fell to the wayside and languished. The year after his passing, however, I approached the park district (District 10 Como Community Council, St. Paul Parks and Recreation) with the offer of reviving the event by leading new Como Park Tree Treks of my own. They agreed, giving me an opportunity to carry on my dad's legacy in the park while also sharing my own deep, enthusiastic love of trees. Not long after, it seemed logical to expand the tree signage project, setting a goal of increasing by more than double his initial 18 signs to offer a total of 38 tagged species.

This is why I find myself, almost two years after my dad's death, shuffling about on my hands and knees beneath the large green leaves of the basswood tree, companionably searching for a hot-dipped galvanized nail with my new friend, Susan Jane. She is from the park district's Environment Committee, and her advocacy for the tree tag expansion was essential to its revival. When the budget was approved for purchasing tree signs, I was thrilled. Right away in spring, Susan Jane and I arranged a day to make a tree survey and set about choosing suitable trees for the expansion. We enjoyed getting to know each other. That day we singled out as many trees as we could, but a few loose ends still remained to be tied up. So, in early September, I completed the survey to get ready for the two days ahead of us we've allocated for matching up the stack of signs we ordered to their respective trees. And as I go through the morning on this first day of tree tagging, there is an inkling inside me that my engagement with the park is somehow part of my grieving process, somehow combines a celebration of my father's life with a continuation of my own new mission. As such, it is the framework for this story.

Before moving on from the basswood to the next tree, I glance down once more in hopes of spotting that dropped nail, but Susan Jane says she'll look for it later when she walks her dog. Then, from out of the blue, she asks me a question that all at once stabs at my heart. We aren't always willing to see what our psyche knows deep within until we are caught unawares. Under this particular tree species of such family significance, her question instantly propels me onward and forward along my circle of grief, searching to understand that place where my grief and my dad's legacy intersect. Susan Jane asks, "Do you ever feel your dad's presence now that he's gone?"

She had known my dad from several years serving together on the District 10 Environment Committee. Still, while this question comes naturally and genuinely from her, it is also unexpected. Pausing in surprise, I look up, feeling my heart clench a bit.

"No," I say immediately. Then, feeling the need to clarify, add, "You mean by doing Tree Treks and all this tree tagging stuff?"

"Yes," she says, "or just anywhere?"

"No, not exactly here today or anywhere. I mean, I didn't even know that he did Tree Treks; he didn't really talk about it, and I only found out later. We shared a love of nature, so I do feel his presence here in the park sometimes."

It feels like a weak answer, but then some deeper knowledge suddenly rises from within me, a geyser of truth welling up tears in my eyes. I see in that moment many moving parts of the last year of my dad's life coming together. That spring day at Mayo Clinic sitting next to him during the cancer diagnosis, my body tensing, knowing before my mind did what was to come. Later that same weekend on my drive back home, alone in the car, grief rising up from some primal place within me into uncontrollable, unbidden wails that reverberated against the windshield and roof. During that ensuing summer's months of chemo treatment and other follow-ups, many opportunities arose for close, unlooked-for moments of deep companionship and support that I knew, even if I didn't think of it consciously, were some of the last times we'd share together.

"I'd like to tell you more sometime," I say aware that the intense emotions within me won't let me elaborate at the moment. In an attempt to recover, I draw in a breath and think of something else to say instead. "For a while, I didn't even dream about him at all," I go on. "Lately, though, I've started to have more dreams. Two weeks ago I dreamed he was holding this interesting-looking, oppositely branched stem that had two leaves, and looking at it in a puzzled way, turning it this way and that. The leaves were very large and broad, sort of like flags fanning out on each side. 'Do you know what species this is?' he asked me. 'No, but let me ID it for you, Dad. Here, give it to me.' He did, and there was a sense of shared relief that passed between us as he handed it over, a feeling of rightness that I was taking it. That was the dream."

"That's interesting," Susan Jane muses. "I like how it fits in with what you're doing here in the park, carrying on his legacy."

"I guess you're right."

But that is not what I want to tell her. What I want to say is so vital to me that I need to wait first for the right time and maybe even to set it down in words, this complicated exploration of my deep feelings of grief and loss that perhaps, somehow, only trees will be able to help me translate.

Trees have much to share with us beyond shade, oxygen, wood products, food, and their beauty. Living alongside us as we grow and age, sometimes for our entire lifetimes, they calmly and quietly connect us to those who came before us and to those who will come after we are gone. Trees are always available to hold our memories, joys, sorrows, and major life events in their strong branches while we attempt to explain ourselves.

They offer us a way to begin.

I later learned another story about our family and the basswood from my sister, Anne, as the two of us stood outside, caught in a rainstorm. Anne had come to our childhood home to begin her week's caregiving duties to my mom in her turn after my week was completed. Ever since my dad's passing, my brother, Andrew, had moved in as primary caregiver with the five of us siblings giving him regular breaks throughout the year, sometimes for a month. In a symbiotic relationship mutually beneficial for everyone, Andy has been helping her get meals, maintaining the house, taking her to appointments and receiving room, board, and a stipend in return. Without someone living there and running the household, my mom couldn't live at home because her dementia would preclude that. My mom knows us all, plays Scrabble, and compulsively turns off every light in the house or the stove if one of her children leaves them on. Because of her severe short term memory loss, the best thing for her has been to remain in the home she has known and loved for over 50 years. It is no small thing to be able to move effortlessly through a space her body remembers, to spend her days knitting caps on the couch, doing crosswords on her beloved front porch all the while knowing the ins and outs of the dishwasher, bedroom, and nighttime path to the bathroom.

When Anne arrived for her week of caregiving, I stayed on a few days extra and scheduled an autumn Como Park Tree Trek. My sister was unable to attend, but afterwards, I took her on a private Tree Trek through the park. We didn't get far before the weather changed, the skies opened up and it just poured. Too far from the car to turn back, we took shelter under a Norway maple, the closest tree with big leaves. Between the raindrops and shifting around in a fruitless attempt to find the driest way to wait it out, we talked.

She told me the experience reminded her of a trip to Poland she had taken with my parents and another sister two decades previously. In a rainstorm just like this one, there was nowhere to go but under a nearby tree. The four of them had found themselves taking shelter under a little-leaf linden, the European version of American basswood, beloved in Poland. The intimacy that sprang up between their little family group standing in the rain beneath that little-leaf linden mirrored what my sister and I shared beneath the Norway maple. We began to bring up remembrances of our family and childhood. As we talked, it surfaced that neither of us knew the other had oftentimes climbed to the top of the Norway maple that grew high and majestic on our home's front lawn (a tree now deceased and replaced with, of course, a little-leaf linden!). We learned we both had spent many hours up top that Norway maple. I had never known this about her, and vice versa! My sister then shared with me that after they returned home from the Poland trip, she told my dad how hurt she had felt during some very awkward, unhappy moments she'd experienced on that trip.

"How did he respond?" I asked.

"Dad turned to me and said in an astonished voice, 'But what about the rainstorm underneath the linden tree? Wasn't that great?'"

With rain pouring over us in a drenching downpour from which the Norway maple could no longer protect us, she told me her answer to my dad, that this experience was, indeed, the highlight of that trip and a precious memory. She couldn't disagree.

What a lovely thing to carry forward!

Along with the stories we tell about trees, every tree we come across has its own story waiting to be heard as well. Each species is distinctive in its own way, with its own culture, unique characteristics, and morphology. When we start looking at trees, really observing, we can find so much more going on behind the scenes than we ever realized—the drama, courtship, reproductive ways, and evasive strategies. Scientists have even found that trees communicate with each other underground through ectomycorrhizal relationships between fungi and tree roots.

Learning what stories trees have to tell has enabled me to move through my grief after the loss of my father. This man, who also loved trees, would completely understand when I state that in listening with both heart and mind to what trees have to say, I have become their storyteller as well.

Chapter 2

Spruce

(Genus *Picea*)

Transformation

Spruce species native to North America run the gamut from the cold-loving boreal spruces of the north (white spruce and black spruce) to the much more heat-tolerant (listed as Endangered) Chihuahuan spruce of Mexico. Red spruce is also boreal but diverges by staying east, from the Maritime Provinces, through the Adirondacks, and venturing southward only in areas of upper elevation. In the western Canadian provinces and west coast states are Engelmann spruce, blue spruce, Sitka spruce, and the elusive (listed as Vulnerable) Brewer's spruce. Native to South Dakota, Black Hills spruce is a naturally occurring variety of white spruce (and South Dakota's state tree!). Of all the spruces, Sitka spruce is both the fastest growing and the tallest. Black spruce, a slow growing denizen of nutrient-poor peat bogs, boreal forests and wettish lowlands, has the smallest cones. Norway spruce, a nonnative, takes the prize for producing the largest cones.

To go along with his 18 tagged trees, my dad and his team created a map that could be printed from the district website. Instead of the old way of relying on visual map markers, our new map uses GPS technology from dropped pin locations taken at each tree. The first map included only one species of spruce. In our updated version, we are adding two more spruce species. Our task for the next two days is to affix as many of the new tree tags from our recent order onto as many of the designated trees as we can. Susan Jane and I now cross the pedestrian bridge en route to the next group of trees on our list, the spruces. As we walk, she asks me another one of her perfectly natural questions that puts me at a loss for words, perhaps because once again, I think my answer will not be the expected one.

"Did your dad teach you about trees?"

"Not exactly, no," I say, then add, "You mean to the point where I'm leading Tree Treks and all that?"

"Yes. I was just wondering how you learned? How long have you been doing this?"

"Not long, really," I laugh. "I love trees, but I didn't learn about them in the scientific way I do now. It was more like—is it deciduous or an evergreen? Of course, I knew much more than that, but until recently, for me that was good enough!"

"Hmm," she says, interested. Again, I feel the need to explain more.

"Tree Trek was something new for my dad, something he took up after he retired."

"He worked with plant diseases at the University, right, with fungi?"

"Fungi, yes, on badly stored grains, and it was very specialized research. For the park project, he got help from someone to teach him about tree identification and their diseases—kind of like what I'm doing now learning from my own resources. I became a Minnesota Master Naturalist volunteer almost two years ago, so not too long ago. It's a newly discovered passion that has pulled me in, and I just love doing this, sharing what I know with others."

"No, that makes perfect sense," she says intently, "and you're good at what you do. You found something you love."

As we finish crossing the bridge, the spruce trees come into view, nicely situated on a wide expanse of rising ground across from the parking lot. To their left, atop the hill, the native western species grow, heralded first by a tall Douglas-fir tree at the hill's crown.

"Just look at the beautiful Douglas-fir up there," I exclaim, pausing a moment. "Isn't that one gorgeous?"

"Oh, it really is! That's one of our previously tagged trees from your dad's map, isn't it?"

"Mm-hmm," I nod absently, my thoughts drifting to my dad and his admiration for that particular Douglas-fir. We gaze at the tree a moment, then continue on our way to the parking lot. About halfway across, I stop again, pointing out three spruce trees straight ahead, not far up the hill.

"Those are the spruces I'd like to ID," I explain. "I didn't show you this before, but from left to right there's blue spruce, Norway spruce, and white spruce, all three growing right next to each other. What do you think?"

From our vantage point below, the silhouettes of these spruces stand out beautifully against the sky. All three are clearly different species when you view them from a distance. The variability in their overall shape and growth pattern is very apparent. Of course, up close their needle color and cone variations also provide great ways to distinguish them.

"Young blue spruces," I continue, "grow in a more symmetrical, pyramid shape. Older ones like that one on the left start to become stragglier, more open limbed, which I think is very attractive as well. I do like them!"

"I like blue spruce, too," says Susan Jane. "Blue spruce was my dad's favorite."

"I remember you saying that last spring on our tree survey."

"He always liked the blue spruces," she repeats, smiling to herself, lost in her own memories of her dad. "Let's do your idea. It's an excellent way to compare and contrast when the trees are located so close together like that."

We continue up the rise toward the three spruce trees.

"When I picked these, I was imagining a class of school children standing in a group with all three species right in front of them at the same time," I say as we approach the trees, "so they can see the variations between them all at once, like, for example, how the cones differ so much in shape and size."

"Exactly!"

"I love the thought of connecting people to trees like this," I say.

Spruce trees are classified in the genus *Picea*, of which there are more than three dozen species growing all over the world. Each needle (leaf) of a spruce tree is attached singly to the branch on a small peg-like structure, closely spaced in a spiral around the twig. Spruce needles are squarish, tend to be stiff and sharp, and can smoothly roll between your fingers.

When Erling and I moved to our home in Aitkin in 1992, a white spruce (*Picea glauca*) was living on our front lawn, towering fully mature and very enjoyable to us until its passing from old age in 2015. Remnants of its former glory remain, however, in the form of several stumps cut from the massive trunk. After letting the stumps dry for a week or so, I peeled the bark off four of them and made decorative, sturdy bases for two lakeside fire ring benches at our family's cabin. Three more of the stumps now provide a rustic, sturdy base for my dad's memorial bench, made by Andrew and Julie, which also occupies a special place on that land. The remaining base of the tree trunk we left tallish and intact where it still rises up about 25 feet. The hope is that it might invite more wildlife to the yard, even if just as a perch for a bird.

Every part of a spruce tree has provided people for millennia with gifts, from root to tip. Indigenous Peoples traditionally use the fibrous roots to sew pieces of birch bark together to form products ranging from baskets to traditional birch bark canoes. The buds are high in vitamin C as well as carotenoids and minerals. Branch tips of some species are traditionally used in the brewing of spruce beer or steeped to make a nutritious, medicinal tea. The resin, that sticky substance oozing from evergreens, is antiseptic and can be used as a healing salve. Spruce resin can be processed to make pitch for glue or waterproofing, and into rosin for violin bows. For recreational chewing, resin (typically from red or black spruce) at one time was boiled down into a popular product called spruce gum until modern materials replaced it. The long fiber structure of spruce wood is valued in making paper. Spruce heartwood reverberates in its own special way, as do many other species of wood used in musical instruments. A piano's inner soundboard, for example, is usually made of spruce, as was my first guitar—a fact that warmed me to it immediately, knowing what tree it came from. Forest creatures also enjoy the seed cones and buds of spruce trees for daily sustenance.

Clearly, the gifts from spruce trees manifest in many ways. The preciousness of each individual tree, juxtaposed with the practical transformation from its harvest is an easy sort of alchemy, repurposing what was already gold into another form of the same. Our yard's white spruce tree also symbolizes my own transformation from a person who described everything with evergreen needles as a "pine tree" into a serious naturalist concerned with the correct genus identification of conifer species. It's an important distinction to make! (Though the fact that spruce, pine, larch, and fir are all classified in the Pine family probably adds confusion.) Not long ago, I would refer to our yard's white spruce with comments like, "That pine tree looks so beautiful today!" or "Do you like where I hung the bird feeder on the pine tree?"

To which my husband would reply, "Ahem. It's a spruce."

"Oh, right. Whatever!" Heedless and unknowing, I went on repeating the mistake over and over again.

Then, about six years prior to leading my first Tree Trek, I began to take daily walks, usually just about at the time the sun rises off the horizon. These early morning walks included moments of what I called "Vitamin Sunshine" and involved lifting my face to greet our planet's star. Getting outside daily into the natural world quickly became a delightful practice that helped me find calm and meaning during a challenging period of my life. I enjoyed the light dancing through my closed eyelids, letting the sunshine do its healing work. Three years into this routine, I began to notice nature around me in a new way. I began to observe subtle changes of seasons through which plants, animals, birds, elements, insects, weather, and all things unseen (microbes, energy) interact to make a world unto itself—our universe of life around which all things revolve, which includes all of us. Another word for this is phenology. Structures. Patterns. Seasons. Changes. As a working visual artist, my approach had always centered on capturing nature's beauty through a painter's understanding of the way light, shadow, and reflection play upon a landscape. Increasingly, I was coming to value knowing nature from a naturalist's perspective, wanting to identify plants and understand their place in the scheme of things uncovered by scientific inquiry. A balancing act occurred in my mind between the beauty of nature and the scientific knowledge base, each enhancing the other and uniting me profoundly to it through both heart and mind. Nowadays, greeting a tree either by its common name or its Latin nomenclature, in addition to knowing whether it is male, female, or both, has become my modus operandi—a friendly way to approach and get to know other living species with which we share planet Earth.

About four years into these morning walks, my thoughts began to coalesce around moments of creative observation connecting nature, ideas, and life experience. Every day brought a new chance encounter leading to a new idea that was meaningful. Not knowing what it would be, I left myself open to whatever would come, content in the knowledge that my daily ramblings would lead to discoveries waiting to reveal themselves. All I had to do was walk and observe what presented itself in that moment, that day. Even now, the thought of this simplicity available to every single person at all times brings a calm smile to my lips. A blue jay calling. The wind against flower faces turned a certain direction toward the sun exactly the same way as mine when I get Vitamin

Sunshine! Dewdrops scattered amidst deer prints in the sandy road beneath my feet, a trail leading … somewhere. In time, a strong urge came over me to write down these observations, and so I began to do so, usually immediately upon returning home before I would forget the experience and its feelings. Often, the connections come for me through the creative act of writing with nature as my muse. While learning, for example, about a particular flower that caught my eye, I would enter a realm of thoughtful reflection. Writing (or journaling) is one way we can come to know ourselves, one way we can meet our own inner wisdom, and perhaps over time even discover a new path or passion we might encourage ourselves to follow.

Creative writing has always appealed to me. As a younger woman, I began sharing my poetry with my dad during the time I worked as a secretary at the University of Minnesota, where he was a faculty professor. Often, I would send him my latest poem through the intercampus mail system addressed to Dr. Chet Mirocha, Department of Plant Pathology. It was a fun way to connect, even though I lived in the same city and would visit my childhood home quite often. In later years when I moved away, email or U.S. Mail became the vehicle for transmission, and it was a good feeling to know that he appreciated each one of my poems. Through the decades, he saved them all in a folder in his file drawer.

My writing evolved over time. My reflections from my nature rambles are longer, poetic, with a well-researched science component, all of which my dad could relate to. He possessed a poet's heart and sensibility in his inner life as well as being a scientist in his career. For me, these writings exemplify a personal transformation that began to pour out of me in the spring of his final year. Was it a coincidence? Did some sort of transference occur between us? Why do we follow a certain passion or inspiration that arises from within? A small part of my motivation for sending him these nature writings over that last summer of his life was to entertain him, knowing he wasn't always feeling well. Like with my poems, I knew he'd appreciate these writings.

Over that summer, he answered every one of my blog posts with a short comment or insight, and this nurtured our closeness. With their naturalist twist, these posts very much appealed to his own love of nature and lifelong learning. So yes, that historical connection with him was part of my transformation, but a larger part involved listening and following the inclinations coming from my heart. I was simply exploding with the joy of learning and discovery through the biology, botany, and ecology of the world around me.

That autumn, two months before my dad died, the lady selling mushrooms at our local farmers market mentioned that her daughter had trained as a Minnesota Master Naturalist through UMN Extension and was teaching a class on medicinal herbs. That seed, once planted in my consciousness, grew and pulled at me, would not let go. It was unexpected—so unlike my previous inclination to view classifying things as taking the life out of them. "Just enjoy it for its beauty" had once been my motto. That changed. My dad, when I told him I was thinking of doing this, just loved the idea and encouraged me to go with it.

"But just maybe," I hedged. "I don't know where all this will lead really, or if I'll actually do it."

Two months after my dad died, I found myself training as a Minnesota Master Naturalist.

I still ask myself, was there a bit of magical transference of knowledge and love of trees going on toward the end of my dad's life? Possibly, and it's fun and comforting to think of it that way. But honestly, that love of trees, learning, and nature has always existed within me. All I know is that exposure to nature and then writing about it transformed gold residing deep within me into another form of the same. When we find such things that allow personal growth and possibly even healing, it is truly something for which to be grateful.

Now, as Susan Jane and I draw near the blue spruce, I hitch up my bag of nails and adjust the hammer from banging against my thigh. As the only tagged spruce tree on my dad's original map, locating the exact tree he chose so many years ago among the many in the general area was as essential to Susan Jane as it was to me. We both wanted to stick as close as possible to Chet's original map, but that blue spruce proved elusive to find. The prior spring on our survey we searched and searched without success. There are so many spruces on that hillside! Assuming time had weathered away its tag, we had gone ahead and added blue spruce to our order list (which included all the new tags as well as necessary replacements), leaving the choice of which tree for later. Then, two weeks earlier when I was alone in the park finalizing things for this day, I stumbled by accident upon the original tagged blue spruce tree that went with the map. How I missed this tree before is a puzzle; it grows in plain sight along the sidewalk, but I guess I just didn't look closely enough. I've been waiting for this moment to share my discovery with Susan Jane.

"Look, Susan Jane," I say, leading the way up a few steps until we stand right under the huge, draping branches. "I want to show you something."

"Blue spruce," she says, admiring up close the attractive branches with their bluish needles reaching out in all directions but not noticing the weathered scraps of old tag.

"Yes, but there's something else."

I bring her closer so that we're standing right in front of the trunk.

Susan Jane is still not reacting, not making the connection. In a sudden insight, I realize she might not know that the first generation of tags looked much different from later tags. They were small and made of red painted metal, with embossed letters stating both the common name and its binomial nomenclature (*Genus/species*). They were experimental, I think, and there weren't very many of them. The ones my dad switched to are larger and more formal—the same brand Susan Jane and I are using. These are sized 4x6 inches, composed of white laminate, and printed with species information along with a line drawing of the leaf.

"See?" I run my fingers gently over the remnants of the red metal label that remains affixed to the trunk. "This is one of my dad's original tags." My voice is a little lower, somewhat breathless. "The one from my dad's original tree map. You can still see some of the embossed writing on it. We've got his blue spruce. This is it!"

"Okay, but I don't recall ever seeing this kind go through the committee. Maybe it was before my time, but I don't know for sure who put these on."

My hunch is confirmed but I keep it to myself, leaving her with a bit of that sense of mystery I've been feeling—even though I *do* know who put these on!

"Anyway," Susan Jane continues, "This is definitely the tree to do because it was tagged before, whoever did it."

She starts matter-of-factly shuffling through the signs in her tote, looking for the replacement.

I can still feel that first rush of joy coursing through me as I look at those bits of faded red metal on the tree. How my heart leapt when I first discovered them! The blue spruce of my dad's original tree map. The words of the tree name are still partially intact, but most of the tag has stripped away through the years. Encountering this remnant was (and still is) like coming face to face with my dad, discovering him again if only for a moment and from another time, as if our paths have crossed by chance in the park and I am catching him in the act of doing something he loved. So, too, here I am now doing the same activity, and it feels like reaching back in time and pulling him into the present along with me.

"That's strange," Susan Jane says. "I can't find it. We must have left it off the order by mistake!"

"Oh? Wow! That's too bad."

"I think we need to follow up," I propose. "It's your dad's favorite, and this tree was on the original map."

"Yes, let's go ahead and order another one," Susan Jane agrees. "Someone can come back anytime to attach it when it comes in…"

"…since it's marked already where to put it," I complete her sentence with a smile, "right over the remnants of the old one!"

As we walk away, I look back once more at the tiny bits of metal and two rusty nails holding them, now deeply embedded in the tree trunk. There is nothing I can do about removing them. They may always remain in the tree. With a plan of action now in place, a sense of completion fills me. My dad was here, and that knowledge is comforting.

For the moment, that seems to be all that matters.

Chapter 3

Maple

(Genus *Acer*)

Separation and Hanging On

Some maples have very practical names—red, silver, sugar, black. In contrast, striped maple of eastern North America into Canada is also known as moosewood, goosefoot, whistlewood, and snakebark! A western species of Acer, *Rocky Mountain maple, has a native range much larger than its name implies though it does stay exclusively west. Vine maple appears mostly in the Pacific Northwest along with bigleaf maple whose range extends farther down the west coast. Rarest of all the maples is Mexican sugar maple. Different species of sugar maple grow all across the continent. Native to the inland West is bigtooth maple, a.k.a. western sugar maple, while the southeast coast through Texas is home to southern sugar maple. Box elder is a maple, too, and has the widest distribution from Canada, through every state, and into pockets of Mexico. Two exotic invasives are Norway maple and Amur maple, introduced as ornamentals but now naturalized and competing with native species.*

Susan Jane and I make our way toward the trunk of a red maple (*Acer rubrum*). Two red maples, actually, are companionably growing about 20 feet apart from one another, adjacent to a small shrubbery on one side and a quiet street along the other. I've selected the tree closest to the street for tagging. It's a bit off the beaten track, but that makes it all the more fun for self-guided tree trekkers to search for. I explain to Susan Jane that my basic reasoning to tag this one is location. Though not growing right next to each other like the tagged spruces, two other maple species on the tour grow in this general area, sugar maple (*Acer saccharum*) and Amur maple (*Acer ginnala*), providing nearby contrast and comparison opportunities in this big park.

Maples are one of the few trees in the plant world that present their buds (and therefore their leaves) growing opposite one another along the branch in pairs. Most tree buds come out of their twigs in an alternate pattern, growing in a staggered way up the branch. Opposite branching is one useful way to ID a maple in the wintertime when there are no leaves to help. After determining whether branch buds are alternate or opposite, a winter tree trekker can then move on to observe the dormant buds and also what is referred to as "leaf scars." For, when a leaf separates from its twig in autumn, there remains at the zone where it detached a permanent mark unique to its species. The tiny dots within the leaf scar correspond to the ends of the leaf's vascular tissue that carried nutrients from the twig into the leaf during the growing season. These dots are called the bundle scar, also unique to the species. Their arrangement playing within the shape of the leaf scar can inspire the imagination to find smiles, faces, or shapes.

This being early autumn, we still have plenty of leaves hanging around to entertain us.

"The sugar maples turn color first," Susan Jane remarks, "at least, they have this year."

It's true. We have just come from the sugar maple grove, and one or two of those trees are gloriously shining red against the blue sky of this lovely day, juxtaposed against the freshly mown, green grass. The leaves of our red maple, in contrast, are still fluttering green above us in the breeze. I tap in the sign for *Acer rubrum*, and we pause to look back and enjoy the vista view of the sugar maples spread out below.

Beauty surrounds us in every direction. Green tones mingle their leafy notes with the first tints of fall color, or, as in the current display of the sugar maples, blazingly scarlet with intention. Every tree has their season, and maples are particularly striking in autumn. Leaves change color as the days become shorter and temperatures cooler. At that point, the leaves stop photosynthesis and start sending their remaining nutrients down into their roots for winter storage. The green fades away, leaving the other color components to dazzle. Yellows come from the protective carotenoids that were always there. Reds and oranges form in the autumn from anthocyanins in leaves of species more sensitive to sunlight; these vary from year to year in response to any given season's temperature and cloud conditions. Cool, sunny days produce the most brilliant foliage.

While the magnificent display of reds, yellows and oranges easily draws people out for leaf peeping in the fall, spring is also a time when maples demand attention. Minnesota is home to an abundance of sugar maples, with a sugaring season typically beginning in March and lasting well into April. Eastward, maple syrup production increases due to ideal weather conditions and climate. Quebec is the highest producer of maple syrup in the world, with Vermont as top producer in the United States. When temperatures drop below freezing at night and rise into the forties during the day, that freeze-thaw pattern creates the best conditions for sap to run. From spouts tapped into individual trees for collecting sap in buckets to haul back to the sugar shack, to elaborate tube lines running from tree to tree feeding directly into sugar houses for commercial processing, sugarmakers watch for signs of the first sap run, ready for collecting.

Any *Acer*—red maple, silver maple, box elder and so on—has a sweet sap; it's just that sugar maple has the highest concentration of sugar. This means it takes less sap to boil down into syrup or further to make maple sugar. Regardless of species, it takes a lot of sap to produce syrup. A University of Vermont study showed that an individual sugar maple tree's sugar content varies not only annually, but also fluctuates within the same season. Tricky in that it's not always predictable! What is clear is that spring weather patterns determine the timing for collecting sap during the crucial four to six weeks of maple season, depending on the region. Timing is everything.

Weather was a key element of my dad's daily life. As an adult, he began to follow the weather news avidly because his passion was outdoor recreational activities, especially biking and skiing, which of course are weather dependent. In time, he habitually enjoyed watching weather both on the news and outside. This interest in weather was mutual between him and my husband. Erling's days have always revolved around weather. What started as a farm boy outdoors watching changing conditions evolved into a need-to-know approach for our outdoor art fair business—an enterprise highly dependent on weather. The difference between my dad's approach and my husband's boils down to, on the one hand, a forecast giving more of a short term look vs. a fuller understanding of how and why all the bits and pieces fall into place to create a bigger weather picture. Erling's approach is the latter. During college, he took a science course that included a section on meteorology, found himself naturally drawn to that subject, learned the science behind it, and now integrates that knowledge into his daily observations of patterns and systems. The big picture of weather, in other words, is one of his passions. For these reasons, among the three of us, we began to refer to my husband as the "Senior Weatherman" and my dad as the "Junior Weatherman," which gave us a lot of fun over the years.

In late fall of 2019, when our family found ourselves abruptly thrust into full-time caregiving at home for my dad, we worked together to help him go through hospice. Once it became clear that he was very ill, I only left his side once to get things in order at home for a short, three-day stint. The rest of the time, I put my life on hold to be with him.

"I'm not leaving," I said when he resisted and questioned my canceling of art shows. There was that tone in my voice that I meant what I said. "I'm only going home for a few days, and then I'm coming right back and I'm not leaving."

"Okay," he said meekly.

During those few days that I went home, I used a photo I'd taken of some red maples on the boulevard in front of my parents' house to write a nature blog post about a morning walk. As usual, I emailed it to him that same day. My sister, Julie, was with my dad during this time, preparing to take him to a Mayo Clinic visit, and I asked her to read him the post in case he was too weak to check email.

Of course, I couldn't know at the time this would be the last writing of mine that he would ever know.

Upon my return, he and I sat on the futon couch upstairs in the TV room where he was parked most days. He told me he'd enjoyed the latest post, that it got him thinking. He taught me about abscission, the botany term for the biological process of how a leaf's petiole (or stalk) lets go of its twig so that the leaf falls to the ground in autumn. That, of course, is how leaf scars are formed. Going beyond the cessation of photosynthesis which makes leaves change color, abscission, he explained, is a complicated process with chemicals and hormones that cause the base of the senescent leaf's petiole to thin and release.

"What's a senescent leaf?" I asked.

"It doesn't have to be a leaf," he said. "Abscission can happen to any unneeded organ or part. Senescent just means old or used up, ready to go."

I did not voice my thought that he himself was like a senescent leaf, mostly because it was not a conscious, concrete thought. It half formed in my mind, though, and hung in the room changing colors conspicuously to get my attention, but I did not want to take notice.

All this dying stuff was something I had no experience with. My dad did, though. For decades, he had volunteered in a hospice program. He knew what was happening more than we all did. He was preparing himself.

Ironically, his favorite tote bag he carried to organize his notes sported big blue HOSPICE letters across the middle. He'd received it while volunteering; it often drew a second look from medical staff who entered his exam room. During our last visit, given the latest update of results, my dad told his doctor and her assistant that it was time to go into hospice. A heavy, almost painful sadness draped a cloud of impending tears over all of us. For a few moments, no one spoke. To break some of that tension, I drew their attention to my dad's tote and said lightly, "Well, at least now your hospice bag makes sense, Dad!"

It offered some joviality to help maintain our collective composure, in contrast to a few minutes later when we were by ourselves waiting in the lobby for the clinic valet to bring around our car. I was near the front windows keeping an eye out for it when I looked back at my dad, resting quietly by himself in a chair by the elevator wall. He looked so vulnerable sitting there alone with the reality of his decision, and the sight filled me with the immediacy of the situation. It sunk in how I would lose him soon. I crossed the lobby, crouched in front of him, and said, my voice breaking, "I'm going to miss you, Dad."

"I'll miss you, too." He nodded in his quiet way, holding inside, as usual, all his emotions, though they revealed themselves in his eyes.

When we returned from the clinic, he climbed the stairs for the last time. I didn't know it was the last time, but he seemed to. At the top, he looked around at the physical layout of the rooms in an appraising way and said aloud, "Okay, good. All on one floor. That will work."

With everything in order and "all on one floor," he proceeded to go through the final week of his life. He sat on the futon couch, then took to his bed the way animals retreat when their time is near, in his case bundling up underneath the fluffy down comforter. But he was not all calm, resigned, and practical. He was alternately depressed, hopeless, frightened, demanding, and needy—in other words, human. We didn't know all the physical signs, all the changing conditions that would tell us exactly which way the weather was blowing. Nothing could give us an exact explanation or timing of my dad's own abscission. A senescent leaf lets go slowly without advertising the moment of its release. None of us could know that in less than one week, he would complete the process.

I later went back and edited the last post my dad saw to include the important concept of abscission, increasingly impressed with how science has a name for everything!

October 27, 2019 | Morning Walk Report, Trees

No Separation

A hard frost last night loosened the tenuous connection of maple leaf petiole to twig that has held the leaves fast all summer. In botany, this process of letting go is called abscission. Springtime through now, green leaves fluttered with no separation through storms and languid days alike, sheltering birds from view and shading other creatures passing beneath (such as myself). I look up at the marvelously colored red leaves of the red maple still holding fast to their twigs against the backdrop of blue morning sky. One particular red maple on the boulevard, however, is so frost affected from last night's temperature plunge that it performs an unusual phenomenon for its species. Each leaf on this red maple is all at once helpless to continue hanging on to its twig. Instead of falling a few at a time over days, this tree's leaves are falling all at once in a few hours.

I pause to sit for a while beneath this red maple on its carpet of frozen leaves—reds, yellows, oranges with their lighter undersides intermingled. I listen to (and sometimes feel) the pitter pat of each solid frozen leaf as it drops one by one in a continuous freefall, each leaf randomly taking turns. Unlike the usual soft-drop-flutter-down, this is a solid little thud as each leaf lands. The way they bounce off me in this way makes me laugh, so noticeably hefty and solidly present is each one. The leafy carpet on which I kneel feels chilly, and the warmth of my skin melts them through my pants, making itself known to the frosty leaves, and vice versa. By the end of the morning, all the leaves on this tree will have dropped.

Today, two days later, back home two hours north again, the red oak trees are the sole retainers of leaves—beautiful russets and browns and autumn chestnut colors—while other species of trees have laid themselves bare. Red oak, ironwood, and sugar maple are some of the few deciduous trees that hold their leaves well into winter, called marcescence in botany. The base of a marcescent leaf's stalk withers but retains just enough life to keep the dried up leaf attached until the abscission process completes in spring. Most tree branches, however, now reach denuded arms to the sky. They remind me of the long winter months ahead in which they will continue to look this way.

On second thought, however—not so!

In reality, all trees respond to the weather and will be dressed in an endless array of variants of frosty pearls, whites, and rainbow crystal colors refracting through ice and snow. Weather does not stop, thank goodness. It keeps on coming up with things—some of them very decorative—that remind us of the ever-changing conditions that all living and nonliving things share. As our local weatherman points out, this autumn we will have rain and more rain until the rain turns into snow. This autumn, in particular, has been very wet overall.

Lately, a favorite phrase I've been using in conversation is "The Good, the Bad, and the Ugly," after the epic Spaghetti western film, which seems to sum up many and various situations for me right now. Life presents combinations of the good, the bad, and the ugly, usually all in the same day. Ruinous situations may surround you. Your particular condition in the plethora of constantly swirling human emotions may leave you feeling, for example, trapped and lonely, lost and helpless. Like a video game where you find yourself in the midst of virtual buildings falling down around you. Floods overwhelm the shore. Storm winds threaten to blow you over until you find the center—your center—the eye of calm in the hurricane. You find that everything actually does not focus upon you. Frozen leaves continue to drop quietly down in succession with a gentle pitter-pat in the silence, regardless of whether or not you happen to be in the way. This neutral contact gives you the opportunity to become aware and notice that particular moment where you are, just as the inner calm of your core is always, unflaggingly, urging you to do.

As I write, I recall sitting on those frozen leaves and that moment when I suddenly felt connected intimately with the red maple tree. Breathing in a circle from torso through trunk, back into my own lungs and out again, I felt a stark camaraderie of legs and hands, branches and leaves, head and crown reaching to the sky. Useless thoughts detached and fluttered away until suddenly all the trees around me appeared in a different perspective, as part of me. No separation! Their beauty reaches out for me now, fills my heart with hope and song, and I can almost see the buds that will arise next spring, tender and alive—as am I.

All the weather conditions that arise, that keep the variables changing, moving and repeating through the seasons, provide the natural backdrop revolving through our lives. Weather takes away any illusion of division between me and everything else. No one escapes its effects. Prepared, present, and listening, you will act accordingly, with the extra bonus that if you keep your eyes open, you will (along with everything else) remain naturally awake and on your toes for whatever is coming next.

Chapter 4

Oak

(Genus *Quercus*)

Leaving and Letting Go

Oaks are keystone species in their ecosystems, vital to the diversity and health of the biological communities they support. About 90 species of oak range across North America. Gambel oak of the Rockies heads south into northern Mexico. Garry (or Oregon white) and California black are two oak species among many growing in Pacific Coast states. From gray oak, cherrybark oak, California white oak, and all the various live oaks to our most widespread oak species—white, bur, chinkapin, and red— Quercus *extends across the continent into widely diverse habitats. Live oaks are evergreen. Southern live oak is native to Texas eastward, scrub live oak enriches the desert southwest, and California, canyon, and coast live oaks are native to the far west. All oaks produce acorns—highly nutritious nuts each species presents in its own signature shape, size, and color.*

November 26, 2019 | Morning Walk Report, Trees
Hole in the Landscape

On November 14, my father passed. How can one survive the loss? The hole in one's life, the emptiness in the landscape?

Yesterday, on my morning walk in our small town's city park, I came upon three oak tree stumps adjacent to the playground. They must have been cut while I was away caring for my dad in the last weeks of his life. The unexpected missing oak trees in that particular spot shocked me. Disoriented, I looked around to double check my location, then felt my grief unfold as reality set in.

The oaks I had named the "Twin Oaks," which I wrote about in a post last May, had suddenly become two sheared off stumps, their flat, white faces bared to the sky. Like most other oaks in our park, they were a species called bur oak (*Quercus macrocarpa*), and I had loved them.

Today, when I returned to photograph them, the two Twin Oak stumps were already mounded over with soil from an earthmover redoing the adjacent road. Now they are hidden. Only the third stump remains visible. So fast, already gone. No body. No remains.

My father donated his whole body to science. When the university attendants came to retrieve his body, our family followed the gurney outside and across the front yard to the shiny black university van waiting in the driveway. His funeral procession. Next to the space where his body would slide in was a folded up gurney. I felt somehow relieved to see that side was empty. As the body was placed into the back of the van, a crow cawed loudly nearby. I looked up and saw it flying directly overhead, a sight immensely meaningful and comforting to me. Then the van doors closed. Julie, who has lived in Japan, bowed low in the deepest sign of respect until the van had disappeared from sight. Because that felt right, I bowed low also, then stood with folded prayer hands to forehead in another form of respect, then let my gaze drift upwards again into the sky.

My father had non-Hodgkin's lymphoma, a type of blood cancer that starts in the white blood cells of lymph tissue found throughout the human body. The lymph system is part of the immune system, and also helps fluids move through the body.

The city park trees, some of them anyway, are currently infected with oak wilt. Oak wilt is a fungus that enters the vascular system of the tree (the xylem and phloem fluid vessels), eventually cutting off the tree's supply of water and nutrients. It is a fatal disease. As a plant pathologist, perhaps Dad would appreciate the similarity of oak wilt to his hematology-related disease. Or maybe not.

His life was wonderfully full, a life lived with adventure, doing the things he loved, surrounded by loving friends and family.

So, on flows the river freely alongside the walking path, never stopping, swiftly moving, ever changing. The banks are edged with lacy, beautiful ice forming, cold and opaque.

Like the edges around my heart.

A fat squirrel crosses the path grasping a nut in his mouth to stow away for winter. A chickadee calls out loudly, her vapor breath filling the air with such warmth it penetrates my loneliness and thaws the cold, opaque edges.

Walk on, for wherever you go there will be a path. There are times to simply walk, heedless of direction or which fork to take. Walking for walking's sake can be purposeful in itself, unfolding the way into the labyrinth of your heart and back out again.

There is peace to find in that.

Chapter 5

Northern White Cedar

(Genus *Thuja*)

Healing Words and Gentle Touch

Northern white cedar (Thuja occidentalis) *is truly a tree of the north, preferring the continental climate of its cold and humid native range in the upper tier of the eastern half of the United States into Canada. From Minnesota across to New York state, its range extends northward until it meets tundra. Local pockets grow in states just south of that tier as well as deep into the mountains of southern Appalachia. Western redcedar* (Thuja plicata) *grows tall and sublime in the moisture-rich maritime climate of temperate rainforests along the western slopes of the Pacific Coast Ranges, from northern California to Alaska. Inland populations also prefer areas where moisture is abundant, such as near mountain streams, and can appear as far east as the western slopes of the Rockies.*

Fourteen northern white cedars beckon to me. The group is planted in a semicircle flanking the flagstone seating area that is covered with a white pergola. It is early on the first day of the two-day tree tagging project, an hour before I will search for a nail beneath the American basswood—the tree that begins this story. Susan Jane has not yet arrived. My eyes run over the northern white cedars lined up shoulder to shoulder before me in a continuous line of foliage. Which one to give an ID sign? The park staff would want people to access a tree on either end, not mess around in the middle of the row, and so I choose the one closest to the Lily Pond. The sound of the fountain's spray fanning out over the water accompanies my thoughts, along with birds and the footsteps of early morning parkgoers. The first thing I find in the chosen tree is an empty beer can. Perhaps the owner thought no one would ever find it here, or they just thrust it into the shrubby foliage rather than deposit it in the garbage receptacle six feet away. Go figure. I dispose of the can, then concentrate on the reason I'm here.

Because these particular trees are still young and shrublike, I need to use wire instead of nails for this first sign of the day. The tricky part is getting the sign to hang straight while securing the wire around protruding nubs of twigs and branches. I persist until it looks just right.

"Good luck!" I tell the sign, satisfied and enjoying the fun of doing this. I imagine the coming weather seasons that will rain, snow, sleet, and blow on this soft tree protecting my little sign within it. Exhilarated, I take a photo and text it to our executive director to show him that things are, indeed, in motion! The flat, fanlike leaves of the cedar gently surround the gap in the foliage that I took advantage of, catching the early morning sunlight in shafts of yellow and green. It is a happy sight.

Northern white cedar (*Thuja occidentalis*), or white cedar, is also commonly known as arborvitae. In Latin, *arborvitae* means "tree of life," referring to this tree's medicinal qualities. In 1535, French explorer Jacques Cartier lost several men to scurvy while stranded in the ice-bound Canadian St. Lawrence River, until some First Nations people taught them to boil the bark and foliage into tea. Like spruce needles, northern white cedar leaves contain high amounts of vitamin C. The remaining men survived, and subsequently the tree was introduced into Europe, probably the first North American tree with that distinction. Soon after, it received its intriguing alternate name, "arborvitae", alluding to its "life-giving" qualities.

Thuja also happens to be a very long-lived tree. Given the right conditions, away from the danger of fire, for example, arborvitae can live for hundreds of years, another reason for its grand nom. Several growing on the Niagara Escarpment in Ontario are estimated to be about one thousand years old. Near Grand Portage, in northern Minnesota, a tree sacred to the Ojibwe has been growing out of a huge rock overlooking Lake Superior for over 300 years. Its traditional name translates as Spirit Little Cedar Tree. Others refer to it as the "Witch Tree." To protect this tree from vandalism for generations to come, the

Grand Portage Band purchased the land where Spirit Little Cedar Tree grows in 1989, prohibiting access unless accompanied by a tribal member. Smart move, I think to myself, recalling the empty beer can I've just pulled out.

The diminutive cones of northern white cedar provide a plethora of food for squirrels, ruffed grouse, and a variety of songbirds. I've seen squirrels strip the bark in winter when food is limited. They line their nests with it and also chew the sweet inner cambium layer they have exposed beneath the outer layer of the thin bark. This does not kill the tree, so far as I have observed. Deer and rabbits love to winter browse the twigs and branchlets. Occasionally, I snap off a sprig of *Thuja occidentalis* and toss it into my soup or stew bubbling on the stove. Lots of life surely does thrive in and around these wonderful trees with their flat fronds brushing outwards in waves of gentle caresses.

Northern white cedar is native to Minnesota (our Arrowhead region is just on the edge of its native range eastward) and is classified in the Cypress family (Cupressaceae). It is not, however, a true cedar. If it were, the genus would be *Cedrus*, trees native to the mountainous regions of the Mediterranean and Himalayas. Trees in the *Thuja* genus probably came to be called "cedars" because the pleasant scent of their aromatic wood is similar to that of the true cedars. What's a *Thuja* then? Well, another well-known *Thuja*, western redcedar (*Thuja plicata*) has similarly scaly, flat leaves fanning down on sweeping branches into the dense, shady, and lush temperate rainforests of the Pacific Coast Ranges. Again, not a true cedar either, but at least they are both true cypresses.

Three northern white cedars grow in the front yard of my current home, right next to our front bay window. All winter long I enjoy their green, leafy reminders of warmer months to come. Shade tolerant and cold loving, the dominant range of these trees extends from where I live in Minnesota, eastward and upwards into Canada. South of here, the original, native species is not as common in the wild, but I do often see their cultivars planted in urban landscapes and gardens. In time, climate change may dictate whether these trees can even remain in the southernmost portions of their native range; they may instead migrate northward.

When my dad died, winter was waiting on my doorstep when I returned home, thrusting me immediately into ski season. For the first time, there was no Dad to share my ski report with. Skiing was an activity for which we shared a deep love, especially when he was younger. In his later years, he found bicycling a better fit for weakened knees and age-related cold sensitivity, but he always loved to hear about the trail conditions, weather, and location of my winter sojourns.

Hardy and cold-weather tolerant, northern white cedars remind me of skiing a tracked and groomed trail with my dad, surrounded also with balsam firs and pines decorating the forest with their evergreen needles. When my dad visited us, he would pull my young daughter around the snowy yard, with him on his big grandpa skis and her on her own short skis. He would ski in front of her, holding one ski pole behind him for her to grab onto. In this way they would loop around the front yard. Very fun, and it got her up on her first skis at three years old. Before long, she was holding her own, moving forward on her little skis all by herself and doing very well.

My dad and I strongly connected through our experience of sharing the outdoors in nature together. When I was in middle school, he took up cross country skiing and I learned the sport pretty much at the same time he did. I have a strong memory of being a 13-year-old riding in the car with him past the park's golf course and hearing the excitement, interest, and enthusiasm in his voice as he pointed out two cross country skiers whizzing over the snowy expanse. "Look how fast they can go!" he remarked as we drove past. "Cross country skiing is becoming really popular, and I'm going to try it out. Would you like to learn how to do it?"

Of course I did!

Our first skis were the same, blue wooden ones using a pine tar base, before we switched to the stronger, lighter-weight fiberglass kind that were beginning to appear. More than once those wooden ski tips broke on our adventures out on the ski trails! He always carried a yellow plastic ski tip in his backpack on these trips, used like a spare tire to get back on the trail, an example which taught me about planning and being prepared.

My dad went on to become an expert cross country skier, mountain Telemark skier, skate skier, and ski advocate for the rest of his life. To a lesser extent, we did some downhill skiing as well, often just the two of us, sometimes with my sister, Julie. All of those trips were supportive and memorable throughout my high school years. About that time, he also took up bicycling in a serious way, and we'd take early morning Sunday bike rides together, my fingers turning white in the chill. Cold hands were a sort of theme. More than once when skiing or biking, I had to warm up in his mittens. We bonded through the fun of the trails, learning proper technique together, and bombing the hills that added further challenges and adventure.

We often referred to these times to each other, smiling at the memories certain shared phrases evoked, repeating them more than once. As he lay dying, I thanked him for being my friend, especially during my difficult high school years when I greatly needed that. Our temperaments were similar in many ways, including a feeling of being alone, of having a lone voice. We each had our own separate reasons for this. He may not have taken "the road less traveled" in his own life, but he admired those who did. He approved of the little house I shared with Erling, our down-to-earth way of life struggling as artists. He loved my paintings and bought many.

The two of us, father and daughter, had our ups and downs. One time, on a ski trip we took to the Porcupine Mountains in Michigan, something he said before we left (I don't remember what) made my teenage temper rise so angrily that for hours on the drive I refused to say one word. I just faced the window away from him. Of course, by the time we checked into our motel I had thawed. It was fun to be on a trip together. Out on the ski trails the next day, swishing through the forest, I was ecstatic and didn't want to leave when our weekend drew to a close.

Deep relationships have their hidden wells of pain along with the joys in a dynamic that others cannot see. Ours was no exception. My dad was a '50s guy, as my husband and our culture describes it, or in other words, having all the votes in the family. He was definitely an authority figure head of the household. My mother and siblings and I felt the stress of that. Many times, my mom would ask me to talk him into or out of something. "He'll listen to you," she would plead, her voice almost desperate.

He usually did listen to me.

He was not an easy person to know, somewhat like me, but where I often navigate on the emotional spectrum, he was more practical and rational. His own stubbornness and anger are probably where I get mine, for he definitely had a temper.

A few years before he died, I was sitting with him by his computer prior to dinner, listening as he vented about a minor family situation. While the frustration and anger he vented were perfectly understandable, an unexpected shaft of childhood memory pierced through my adult protection layers, reminding me of the many times I had heard this tone of voice directed at both me and others. Before I knew it, I was crying, telling him how frightened his anger had made me when I was growing up.

"I don't remember," he said in a helpless tone, and I know this is true because when you lose your temper, you do and say things you regret. It's natural and perhaps easier to look at the good you do as a person and as a parent, and so you forget about the bad things which happened in the heat of the moment. Of course, it goes without saying those things don't just disappear for people, especially children.

He took me in his arms then, and I wept wracking sobs onto his shoulder as he comforted me. I hadn't wept this way in a long time. It felt good to let it out.

"I understand about the situation," I explained tearfully, "It's just that your angry tone reminds me of other times."

"I know, I see. I never meant to hurt you. I would never knowingly hurt you and I'm sorry that I did." He said it quietly, almost abashedly, unaccustomed to speaking this directly about feelings. Genuine sorrow, regret, and love formed the soothing balm of these words.

"I know," I said, "I love you, Dad."

"I love you, too," he replied, which were also unaccustomed words for him, though I knew my whole life that he wholeheartedly felt them. That is the most important thing to hold onto, but it is also good to hear those words spoken aloud.

On this and a few other occasions during his last years, as I journeyed on my own personal path, I found opportunities to get some of these things out on the table with him. In the process, despite everything, triumphing over it all was love. Even though we had our issues, the knowledge of genuine love for each other was always there. He was a very loving, good man.

We began to say these words more, repeating them often, especially during his last days.

"I love you," I said, "I'll miss you so much."

"I love you, too."

When you mean them, these are the best words to say to one another. In a way, they are all that matter. They are words full of forgiveness. They offer the gentle, healing touch of northern white cedar fronds, the tree of life. They are the most comforting to hear.

They are enough.

Chapter 6
Douglas-fir
(Genus *Pseudotsuga*)
Finding a New Fit

Douglas-fir's many unique traits set this genus apart from other conifers in the Pine family. From the maritime climate of coastal regions in western North America to the Rocky Mountains south into Mexico, two varieties of Douglas-fir (Pseudotsuga menziesii) *decorate the slopes of their native ranges. Douglas-fir is also cultivated in northern states east of the Mississippi River, from Minnesota to Massachusetts. Though not native here, they thrive and are highly prized for their beauty in landscape design and as Christmas trees. California's southern mountains have their own species, bigcone Douglas-fir* (Pseudotsuga macrocarpa), *distinguished by having the largest cones.*

After wiring the sign onto the northern white cedar, my starting point on today's list, I make my way next to the American elm (*Ulmus americana*). This will be the first tree to receive the effects of my hammer and nails. We are using hot-dipped galvanized nails as recommended by our city forester. I stand in front of the elm with the ID sign poised in one hand and my hammer in the other. Susan Jane has texted me that she will arrive shortly, and I'm glad to continue getting things started alone for these few moments, preparing myself to pound nails into a tree—a first for me. I pause before the elm, then circle around it once.

This is a mature tree with a gigantic, three-foot diameter, serenely emanating a majestic presence. Not for the first time, I let the sense of awe wash through me, standing face to face with an elm that was able to survive the devastation of Dutch elm disease. That plague first arrived in North America in the 1930s, moving slowly east to Minnesota by the '60s, and it changed the landscape of our cities across the continent forever. This tree is a survivor. Almost every elm on our boulevard is gone now, replaced with a variety of species (we learned our lesson) including maple, ginkgo, northern catalpa, honey locust, and disease-resistant elm varieties. When I was growing up in the '60s, the huge American elm from which I gathered perules towered over our postage stamp backyard. On one side a knotted rope was tied for climbing, and on the other—my favorite!—a tire swing provided hours of entertainment. How I loved that tree!

Dutch elm disease is caused by an invasive fungal pathogen and spread by elm bark beetles. As a plant pathologist my dad had the knowledge and access to equipment to try and save our tree using a fungicide injection system. All around the base of the elm he drilled holes and then inserted plastic tubes into them for siphoning a concoction into the living tissue of the tree. In the end it did not work, and that magnificent tree had to come down.

I hesitate. The thought of the wounds I will inflict, however small, has given me pause more than once during the planning phase for this. But, I tell myself, others have done this before me. Pounding nails into trees is what people do, including my dad when he started the first generation of tree tags. So I must go ahead and begin. This includes evaluating the best placement by using both rational thought and how it feels. I find that method works best for me. I walk around the massive trunk again, waiting for that ideal spot to reveal itself.

A tree is not just a flat surface like a bulletin board, where all you have to do is find the empty space. A telephone pole is cylindrical but has no surface variation. Mature bark over a century in age, on the other hand, has grown attractively deep furrows and undulating textures according to its nature, time, the weather, and the flow of its own life. Visibility for the sign is also a factor, but, unlike the goal of placing a flyer in the most conspicuous location, this is a bit more nuanced. Sometimes it feels more respectful toward the tree to use some subtlety. Also, there is the sensibility of the passerby to keep in mind; one need not always choose the most obvious side. Let a walker step beyond their habitual path someday and be pleasantly surprised to encounter one of these. I decide to make this one for the elm tree somewhat hidden. Once I find the spot that feels just right, I draw in a breath, let it out, and tap in four nails, one through each pre-drilled corner. Done! First one complete. Looks and feels good.

The next tree is a silver maple (*Acer saccharinum*), just a bit farther up the walking path. I know right away where to place this one, but I give the tree a couple twirls just to be thorough. This one I label front and center, aware of the wide angles for catching notice. The sign's neutral-colored substrate shines in the morning sunlight. I like how it ostentatiously reflects the eastern light back across the nearby parking lot. I hope it entices walkers to step from the asphalt path, come up close, and read what it has to say.

At this point Susan Jane comes from the parking lot to join me. It is good to see her. Together we head next to the honey locust tree while I fill her in on what's been happening so far. She is in complete agreement with my explanation of the head and heart method for choosing placement, and we soon get into a rhythm of working together. We find that the quality of each heartwood reveals itself in the physical act of nailing. Unlike the abstract idea of each tree simply accepting nails according to plan, in reality, each tree has its own reaction according to its species. We need to find the flattest place, especially on trees with deep, furrowed bark. Some trees have a soft inner wood, such as American elm, while others are hardwoods such as sugar maple and oak. The ironwood tree proves to be the hardest of all, beating out all the others as it vehemently resists our efforts. Nails on some trees bend on the way in and require careful aim or even a new nail. They're also hard to remove. Susan Jane prefers that I do the nailing, but on the ironwood I encourage her to take the hammer and experience for herself how dense that wood feels.

We tackle the balsam fir next, giving the largest one in that grove its new sign.

"Balsam fir is my favorite tree," Susan Jane tells me.

"What makes it your favorite?" I ask, intrigued.

"I like how soft the needles are, how they make the forest such a shady, deep green in the winter. How all kinds of creatures take shelter under their densely-needled branches."

"And eat them!" I add. "Porcupines will gnaw on the bark. Moose and cottontails rely on balsam fir needles by late winter, when everything else is depleted, to help them get through the lean times. Grouse like eating the needles, too, and the seed cones provide food for the animals and birds who are able to get up top to access them."

A rather interesting characteristic of true firs is that their cones neither drop whole from the tree when ripe nor do they hang downwards. Instead, firs present their cones facing upright on branches located in the upper crown of the tree. Each fir cone disintegrates right where it is as the scales with their ripened seeds fall out one by one until only a skinny, bare spindle is left sticking up on the branch. Sometimes squirrels, chipmunks, and several species of songbirds will sit up there and pluck out the seeds, a bit like eating corn on the cob. While these forest creatures may play a small part, fir trees mainly rely on wind for dispersing their seeds from the cone.

Onward we continue, until midday finds us at the rock elm near the district office, at which point Susan Jane says she needs to leave for an appointment. Over the last few hours, she and I have affixed tags to many of the trees. All morning I have been walking. Taking on this effort proves to be invigorating and fulfilling. Joyful rays of energy radiate into every cell of my body as I go from tree to tree. Though I'm tired now, thirsty, and hungry, I just can't seem to get enough of this ecstatic elixir coursing through me. So, I continue by myself a little while longer, coming up with one more area I could visit before taking my midday break. I decide to check out the Douglas-fir hill for a quick inspection of the three ID signs up there from my dad's original map, just to make sure they are still intact and readable.

Approaching the Douglas-fir first, I flashback instantly to almost two decades earlier. My dad was showing me a photo of a tree as we sat around relaxing in my parents' home after dinner. My husband, daughter, and I were staying with them to participate in an art show. This arrangement gave us all a chance to visit, and especially allowed my young daughter to have some precious Grandpa and Grandma time while we were working. The photo he extended out to me that day was printed on a piece of copy paper.

"Isn't that a beautiful tree!" my dad exclaimed as I took the printout from him. "I just took this today."

"It looks like a pine tree," I remarked with my typical aplomb regarding evergreens back then, adding, "or is it a spruce?"

"It's a great exemplar of a mature Douglas-fir," he marveled.

"Oh! I don't know what that is, but it's really nice. I love it!"

Indeed, the tree in the photo presented a towering silhouette rising up gloriously from the top of that hill I mentioned earlier, and quite visible from just about any vantage point.

My pine tree comment, though, accidentally had some merit. I don't mean Douglas-fir is a true pine in the genus, *Pinus,* just the small point that—along with spruce, larch, and fir—Douglas-fir is a conifer in the Pine family. Categorizing this particular species into the Pine family, however, proved tricky for early botanists. The Latin meaning for the genus name that they finally came up with, *Pseudotsuga,* means "false hemlock" because in some ways Douglas-fir does resemble hemlock—but clearly not in enough ways! Douglas-fir cones are much larger (up to 4" long) with other major differences from hemlock cones. The ducts within the wood of Douglas-fir send resin into both the bark and inner wood areas. This is unlike the hemlocks, true cedars, and true firs, where the resin is more or less restricted to the bark layers. Resinous wood is a trait shared with true pines, spruces, and larches; yet Douglas-fir needles are soft and fir-like, dissimilar to those of many pines and spruce. While "fir" is in its common name, it's not a true fir either, hence the use of the hyphen. The seed cones hang downward and fall from the tree intact, the opposite of what the upright, degrading cones of true firs do. Thus, Douglas-fir's name history involved tangled discussions revolving around just exactly what kind of tree it is! Round and round the discussion went between botanists of long ago searching for a way to classify this unique tree. Douglas-fir simply does not fit into any Pine family genus. In the end, botanists created a new genus tailor made just for Douglas-fir: *Pseudotsuga.*

Douglas-fir is its own Pine family person in its very own genus.

One thing that sets Douglas-fir apart from other cone-bearing trees is the cone itself. They have the sweetest, very long-tailed three-part bract at the end of each scale sticking out all over. A visual delight! Whenever I spy one of these cones hanging demurely from a branch or smiling up at me from the ground beneath the tree, my heart gives a little lurch of joy, and I just can't help but smile back.

Two varieties of the main species of Douglas-fir are documented, both nonnative to the Midwest. Coast Douglas-fir thrives in the lush forests of the

Pacific Coast Ranges from British Columbia into California and creates habitat the Northern spotted owl relies on for survival. In ancient, intact forests these regal giants can tower over 300 feet and can live to over 1,000 years. While the bark of mature Douglas-fir is very thick and quite resistant to fire, these trees can succumb to extremely high intensity wildfires in addition to drought, beetle infestations, and disease. The inland variety, Rocky Mountain Douglas-fir, is a smaller tree (about 130 feet in their native range), lives a shorter life, and is also a bit more cold tolerant than the coastal giants. This is the variety we have growing in the park.

For some reason, through the decades after that conversation with my dad, the memory of him enthusiastically sharing that photo of a Douglas-fir has stuck with me. Partly, it shows his obvious love of trees. He never did explain why he was photographing the Douglas-fir that day. Later, I learned about the Tree Trek project, the district sponsors, the Environment Committee's involvement. He wasn't secretive, just not the best at relaying the sequence of information for a more comprehensive view. At the time, I wrote the photo off as his being recently retired with time on his hands, and it wasn't unusual for him to take photos of trees and flowers he admired, so I was assuming that's all this was. Leaving it at that, I had turned my attention to preparing for my art show the next day.

Not until decades later, right after he died, in fact, did the bits and pieces come together at last to complete the bigger picture. People naturally started sharing their memories. Newspaper clippings turned up clues. Someone from the district sent a photo of my dad's favorite tree in the park. My sister mentioned she had gone on one of his early Como Park Tree Treks with her family. Wow! I never knew that! Further research turned up all sorts of information; it was like a black and white picture gone to full, cinematic color. Why had all this flown so long under my radar? Why didn't I make these connections sooner?

I'd known all along my dad was volunteering for tree projects in the park, starting with invasive buckthorn shrub removal. My daughter had told me about Grandpa's tree tags. For 15 years, I might have randomly come across one or two tagged trees on my exercise walks, probably telling my dad how much I liked what he was doing. Beyond that, I didn't look for more information or even think about it. My work took me away on weekends, and Tree Trek was only one Saturday a year. A favorite photo my mom gave me years earlier I knew perfectly well was a Tree Trek promo taken for the neighborhood newspaper. Yet, never before had I noticed that in it, he's wearing a pair of binoculars around his neck! In fact, I ended up using that photo for his memorial service, creating a birch bark frame to surround it. How many people are like me, needing big arrows under a spotlight before they take notice? Understandably, we're distractedly putting energy and effort into making a living. Our focus is directed elsewhere as parents. Sometimes we're just not paying attention.

When I started paying attention, the whole picture swung into a full and complete view. My perspective shifted. Things no longer lined up within me the way I was accustomed, and as a consequence a new picture presented itself. My heart led me to realize that I very much wanted to pick up my dad's legacy and continue where he had left off. Like Douglas-fir, you could say I needed to place myself in a new genus, a genus I never imagined existing in previously. I no longer, however, fit in the former one. Being here now feels familiar and safe, like home. It makes me feel connected and alive. There is no going back!

Each one of us evolves as we go through the many ups and downs of life. Even in the midst of grief and loss, opportunities present themselves for listening, paying attention, taking notice, and following where your own arising inner wisdom leads. As we unlock from the inside and nurture what we find there, a new purpose can reveal itself allowing us to share latent gifts we each possess within us. We may even emerge significantly changed.

The winter after my dad died, upon getting the go-ahead from the park district to revive Tree Trek, I waited for spring to arrive and the snow to melt. Then, I walked my dad's original route using his initial map to locate trees while planning for my own, first Tree Trek. I was so excited! The Douglas-fir from my dad's photo was the first tree I looked for when planning my route. The probability was high that it would prove to be one of his tagged trees. Great anticipation of confirming this filled me as I crested the brick stairway of the park memorial that rests nearby Douglas-fir's hill. That monument was familiar, but then I stepped beyond into an area of the park where I had never set foot before. As a child, I rode my bike around the lake and to the Lily Pond pool below this memorial and often climbed its brick steps, but never had interest in exploring further. As an adult, also, my habitual route for walking took me elsewhere. That day, I felt a great adventure opening up before me upon entering this new realm, and as I drew closer my whole body became energized. Sure enough, there it was. A cream-colored tag with its text and little drawing stood out from the Douglas-fir tree a short distance away, clearly visible in contrast to the dark tree trunk.

The tag winked at me, beckoning me forward like an old friend as if to say, "What took you so long?!"

A rush of happiness suffused me. I avidly read for the first time the tag's information while placing my palms flat against the trunk. I picked up a few cones, planning how I would include these as talking points the next day. Moving beyond the tree, I discovered that the park designers had planted a whole grove of Douglas-firs behind this one, albeit of a much younger generation. Nice!

Since that first in-person acquaintance with Douglas-fir and my introduction into my own, new "genus," I have led several Tree Treks. I've observed the many Douglas-firs popping up in other places throughout this very large park and enjoy imagining future trekkers who will randomly encounter them. My wish is for Douglas-fir cones to continue surprising others with the same sort of magical sparks of delight they ignite in me.

So, here I am now, standing in front of Doug-fir to check out his old sign, just the two of us before I go to lunch. Me and Douglas. Doug's old sign is rather tight to the tree after all, and I begin to remove it. The idea is to reattach the same sign but with longer nails which will provide some growing space between the sign and the trunk in the years ahead. Pulling the old one off, I discover with a shocking jolt of surprise another one of those red metal labels revealing itself from beneath. Just like with the blue spruce, the tag is still attached, except this one is now appearing into the light of day after being covered up for almost two decades. Without a doubt, this small red tag dates back to the year my dad attached it, the year he began leading Tree Treks, the year he took that photo. Again, it feels like he's saying hello.

Smiling, I pull off the unneeded metal tag and stow it away for safekeeping in my zipper pouch. A souvenir after a morning's good work.

CHAPTER 7

Pine

(Genus *Pinus*)

BEING PRESENT WITH GRIEF

Most pines are keystone species in their ecosystems, upon which wildlife largely depends. Eastern white pine, depicted above, shares that role with red, pitch, and Virginia pine in their various native ranges east of the Mississippi River. In a forest type iconic to the Southwest, piñon pine partners with juniper for this. Pines such as longleaf, slash, and loblolly offer habitat—sometimes uniquely—to endangered species in the Southeast. The subalpine tree, whitebark pine (Pinus albicaulis), feeds and shelters wildlife in the mountains of western North America. Bristlecone pine (Pinus longaeva), also subalpine, grows at high elevations of the Southwest and includes individuals thousands of years old. So many native pine species greet us in the Western region! Western white, sugar, Monterey, Parry, and Coulter, to name a few. Similarly, lodgepole pine (Pinus contorta) appears in four varieties from the Pacific coast to the Rocky Mountains. Ponderosa also has geographic variations, and taken with Arizona ponderosa, enjoys the widest range. The rarest species is the Torrey pine.

PINUS IS PRONOUNCED "PIE-NUSS." BELONGING TO THE PINE (PINACEAE) family of conifers, trees in the *Pinus* genus are true pines and produce distinctive female cones with a knob-like structural similarity across species that forms on the ends of their thick seed scales. In botany, this protuberance is called the umbo, a word easier to use than the many words needed to describe it (also useful for crosswords and *Scrabble*!). The umbo is the first year's growth nub protruding from the end of the second year's seed scale. All pines take two years (a few take more) for their female cones to mature after they are pollinated. The umbo can be armed with a sharp spike or prickle. Or the umbo can be flat and small with no prickle, depending on species. In this way, umbos are very useful for identifying *Pinus* species, especially because no other conifer genus has them.

Each umbo on a ponderosa pine (*Pinus ponderosa*) is armed with a sharp prickle, worth a few pinpricks when collecting these attractive cones for a decorative display in a basket or bowl. The needles on a ponderosa grow in clusters of three. In the heat of the sun, the bark emanates a sweet scent reminiscent of vanilla or butterscotch. My dad shared this last fact with me at some time or other, so long ago that I can only recall it as a pleasant memory wafting and lingering invisibly on the air. Ponderosas are one of those long-lived species that can reach 300-600 years of age, sometimes more—a calming thought as I visualize the vast stands of these trees flourishing through the seasons with generations lasting decades into centuries in their native range of western North America.

Having just returned from lunch, I'm feeling refreshed and ready for an afternoon session of tree tagging by myself. I continue past the ponderosas without stopping because the park ponderosa does not need a replacement sign. Their grove looks great. In my pouch, in contrast, is a somewhat weather-beaten sign I removed from the eastern white pine (*Pinus strobus*) on my way to lunch just an hour before. Through the seasons, rivulets of pitch wept down the white pine's length and onto the sign's surface, leaving semitransparent, amber-colored gummy trails. Cleaning the sign off instead of replacing it seemed the logical next step. During lunch, I gave it my best effort to scrub away as much of the pitch as I could without damaging the text. My reward for this is that the surface is now much improved.

For just a little while, the eastern white pine will have to wait for its sign until I can circle back to it later. At the moment, the "head" Scots pine (*Pinus sylvestris*) and I are facing off. Strong and stalwart, this brave leader stands at the top of a gentle slope that descends through an extensive battalion of other Scots pines. This tree is slated to receive a replacement sign (the original having somehow gotten lost), and once again, the remnants of one of those red metal tags my dad placed here almost two decades ago still holds on to its trunk. Unlike the blue spruce and Douglas-fir tags, however, barely anything remains of this one. Just two metal bits spaced three inches apart and each held in by a nail, very easy to miss. This is why neither Susan Jane nor I noticed the tree on our spring foray. In the same way as with the blue spruce, the happy accident two weeks earlier of my stumbling across a previously tagged tree made the choice of which Scots pine to ID out of all these superb ones quite simple.

Pausing a moment, I take in the view of the stately grove of Scots pines before me. In and among the mature trunks, patches of bark on several tree branches are rubbed smooth, being a favorite for young visitors who sling their hammocks between them throughout the lazy months of summer into autumn. In fact, one or two hammocks are out there right now. Still managing to remain at attention, the stand of Scots pine compatriots recedes slowly and peacefully down the slope into the distance, providing food and nests along the way for woodpeckers, owls, songbirds, and small mammals. This is one of the park's many sweet oases. Traffic noise is minimal here. A small area of woods grows somewhat wildly off to the left, acting as a buffer zone from the busy street beyond the walking trail. It is a restful and charming place.

Scots (also called Scotch) pines easily live 300 years or so and are recorded reaching 400 years and older. Their pine needles grow in clusters of two, always in twos, as do red pines, jack pines, and Austrian pines. The thin, scaly bark on the upper branches of older Scots pines becomes a luscious orange color making this pine truly stand out and is a prime way to distinguish it from others of its genus. Frost tolerant and somewhat adaptable to drought, Scots pines are the most widespread conifer in the world. They have historically been a significant part of commercial use for pine tar production, and their resins can be distilled into turpentine and rosin solids. Think of smearing and rubbing pine tar onto baseball bats (or wooden skis bases) and rosining a violin bow, just for starters.

I begin affixing the new Scots pine sign, by now much more comfortable with tapping in nails. It's relaxing here on this pleasant afternoon. Usually I ignore passersby, but unexpectedly, a voice floats over that gets my attention. Sensing that it is surely directed toward me, my head turns that way. A couple is just coming into view about 40 feet away after rounding the bend in the asphalt path. Before this, the buffer zone had hidden them from view.

"A woodpecker!" a man's voice calls over to me.

I'm confused. Are they telling me they saw a woodpecker just now? Or what? Then I see the light as the situation reveals itself. Smiling, I call back to them from my tree, "It probably sounds like that, what I'm doing, doesn't it?"

"Yes! We were surprised to see that it's, in fact, a person!"

I laugh as they continue on, merrily giving the nails a few extra woodpecker taps for good measure.

I love being mistaken for a woodpecker, any time!

Taking respectful leave of our Scots pine, I circle around to the area where the park district commissioned a meditative labyrinth. A round slab here offers seekers of calm a route to slowly open and enter their hearts, an emotional invitation with symmetry etched into the cement. I skirt to the side of the labyrinth. Just past it, a young Austrian pine (*Pinus nigra*) grows right next to the Minnesota state tree, the red, or Norway pine (*Pinus resinosa*). Both pines located here are about the same age and height which presents the perfect opportunity for comparing and contrasting. At first blush, red and Austrian pine are look-alikes. Once you get to know them, however, telltale differences pop out.

Very slightly longer than red pine needles and occurring just like red pines in needle clusters of two, Austrian pine needles are slightly thicker and darker and can also show a slight twist. A useful ID test is to try folding an Austrian pine needle in half. A red pine needle will snap in two if you do this. An Austrian pine needle on the other hand usually just flexes without breaking. Austrian pinecone umbos are armed with a slight prickle that recedes and typically falls off as the cone matures. Red pine umbos are always flat and smooth, even on the first year's growth, and are never armed. Also, Austrian pine bark is darker with a silvery tone, a characteristic that distinguishes it from the reddish plates of the red pine.

Called European black pine in Europe, Austrian pine was one of the first European trees introduced to North America (in the mid-1700s) due to both its beauty and adaptability to all kinds of soil and growth conditions. Their native range is huge, from Europe into Turkey southward to Cypress and into North Africa. Homesteaders on the Great Plains had the most success with seed stock from Austria and the Balkans, which is how Austrian pine's common name evolved here. During the Dust Bowl era of the 1930s, Austrian pine was one of several species—over 220 million trees in all—that the CCC and WPA planted totaling 18,000 linear miles of windbreaks as part of Roosevelt's New Deal project. Starting in 1934 and lasting eight years, the Great Wall of Trees shelterbelt project extended from North Dakota to Texas. Many of these shelterbelts remain intact today or as remnants in need of restoration. Climate change, however, is creating a new stressor to Austrian pines (and other shelterbelt trees), proving more difficult than dust storms to hold out against.

How wonderful it is for me to be speaking about pines! I can't slip up, for these are all truly pine trees. Pines speak to my heart. These two healthy youngsters in front of me, Austrian and red, are too young for tags. Their species' ambassadors grow elsewhere in the park, but I take a moment to step back and enjoy the sight of them before brushing my hands over their bushy pine needle clusters in loose strokes of acknowledgement as I continue past. Soon enough, I come round full circle to the grand pine that speaks to my heart most of all, the eastern white pine. As ever, it radiates its beauty and strength just off the western side of the walking path, surrounded by its companions. Completely unruffled at being left without a sign during the lunch hour, my tree is busy streaming its energy in concert with the breeze playing through its leaves up top, making white pine music. Positioning myself to listen at its base, I gratefully receive any morsels floating down, mere mortal that I am.

Eastern white pine can easily reach 200 years of age, and some are recorded at over 450 years old. The needles feel soft and flexible to the touch in their feathery clusters of five. In addition to joining hardwoods in the rich soils of deciduous forests, eastern white pines also grow well alongside red pines in sandy, well drained soils of riverbanks and open areas. Vast stands of old growth eastern white and red pines often remained intact through the intervention of Indigenous Peoples who used fire culture to keep down the underbrush, aiding both in ease of travel and hunting.

When settlers arrived from England in the 1600s, they marveled at the vast forests of hickory, beech, and sugar maple, out of which the crowns of towering eastern white pines lifted their branches joyously above the treetops. When word of these soaring trees with their massive trunks got back to England, the Royal Navy declared the largest diameter specimens as property of the Crown and marked these trees for exclusive harvesting by carving in a symbol called the King's Broad Arrow. The British naval fleet needed trees for ship masts. Tall trees had become quite scarce in Great Britain, for at one point their own pine resources (Scots pine) had been diminished, and trade blockades for political reasons prevented access to trees in Europe beyond Great Britain. It didn't take long before the Royal Crown took ownership of what they referred to as "mast trees" in the colonies. Anything over a certain diameter could not be used by colonists and instead must be held in reserve to be shipped back to England (fueling fed-up colonists in New Hampshire to instigate the Pine Tree Riot of 1772). Colonists highly valued the wood and used it for basically everything else—bridges, homes, sawmill businesses, furniture—to build this nation. Further contribution to white pine's depletion arrived in the early 1900s on a shipment of white pine seedlings from Europe intended for planting to replace cut trees. The seedlings carried an invasive fungus detrimental to the eastern white pine, white pine blister rust, a pathogen still with us today.

Taking out my freshly spruced up eastern white pine tag, I tap it back into the same nail holes as before but with longer nails this time to space it further from the trunk and allow for growth.

Lifting my gaze upwards at this individual exemplar of its species, I now let my attention flit from branch to whorled branch spiraling skyward. As I do so, my mind wanders back to the day of leading my first Tree Trek, seven months after my dad died. I am standing now in the same place I stood back then, here beside this last tree on my route where I had planned to conclude the two-hour trek. It was an ending, however, somewhat more truncated than I intended, as my emotions sprang to the surface, unbidden beneath this very white pine.

I was just finishing up my remarks when I added, spontaneously, "This is my favorite tree species. I can get really emotional standing beneath mature, beautiful white pines such as this." My eyes welled up with tears. The next moment, I could no longer speak. All I could think to do was to end the talk right there and then.

"I dedicate this Tree Trek to my dad, Chet Mirocha," I managed to say. "Thanks, everyone, for coming."

We slowly dispersed, leisurely making our way back to the parking lot. I walked with a small cluster of women which included Susan Jane who had introduced herself to me during the Trek as being a member of the Environment Committee. My composure quickly and easily recovered, and we conversed about this and that. I clearly remember that moment of suggesting to Susan Jane the idea for an expansion of the tagged trees and her enthusiastic intention to bring it to the committee. After that, we all pleasantly took our leave of one another and returned to our cars.

My thoughts linger on that day. My feelings after that first Tree Trek remain vivid in my mind, not only because I was so happy that my first event had gone well, but also because of what happened next. Yes, it felt great that it was completed and successful, but I was not ready to leave just yet. I had one more important tree stop that day, a visit I'd been saving for afterward that I could only make privately. I wanted to see for the first time my dad's freshly planted memorial tree in the park.

I recall how my route to get to that area of the park was roundabout. First, I took some time to walk peacefully among a few trees I'd just covered with the group. The ponderosa grove drew me because one of the participants had told me about some abundantly fruiting mulberry trees growing nearby. Mulberries are purplish black when ripe. Sure enough, the ripe fruits enticed me to spend a little while beneath their trees overlooking the busy street below. Finally, after replenishing myself on several of these, I felt ready.

It was time to make my acquaintance.

My dad's memorial tree is an eastern white pine I chose and purchased through the city park program with funds a group of loving friends and family donated. As I drew near, the tree beamed its little branches out at me, shining just as beautifully in person as in the photo the city forester had sent me. A living thing to perpetuate my dad's memory, and perfect for him.

"This is for you, Dad," I thought, as I lay on my back next to the tree in the sunshine, and then moved over to do the same in the nearby shade.

Winding down.

I breathed in and out, listening to the chirping birds, the distant voices, the rustling leaves, remaining completely present to my surroundings. My mind had nothing more to think about at the moment, no inner conversation to ruffle things, nothing to plan. Tree Trek was completed; no more energy needed there. My hands were stained from the mulberries with which I had just recharged myself—pigged out on, really. I smiled at the purple-stained palms I stretched above my face.

I lay there a long time.

My heart reached out to my dad through that amiable tree planted in his name. Glowing and healthy, its green needles point upwards as we all must do daily, reaching toward the life-giving sky and allowing our leaves and needles access to whatever comes down into our lives, hearts, and minds. Trees just naturally know how to do this! There is no getting around it for humans, either, although sometimes it isn't easy. Tree roots also naturally know how to go down dark and deep, finding respite and nourishment in the life-giving coolness of the damp mulch and soil below. So must we, although again, it's not entirely easy to become fully aware of the soil in which you are planted where emotions arise that you may want to hide from.

I don't know if it was because I was so open lying there, or so mentally exhausted. Whatever it was, from out of the blue, a myriad of emotions generated within me like rays of light and moved outward spontaneously. Sadness. Relief. Joy. Shame. Grief. They flowed through my body one at a time, and I let them. I did not resist. Each emotion felt enormous until it finished passing through and vanished. I waited for each one to release and then watched them all go.

Exhilarated and exhausted at the same time, I stood at last, got out my car keys, went to the van, unlocked it, took a drink of water; I did all the practical things my body knew what to do that were necessary for driving away from the park. My mind was on autopilot.

It all felt wonderfully good.

Now, with the refurbished ID sign tapped safely back in place, the warm, late afternoon sunlight slants down through the white pine's branches onto my face. Its massive trunk creates a shadow imperceptibly growing longer across the pine needle carpet below. A nearby woodpecker (a real one this time!) is rat-a-tat tapping, calling me back into the present. I'm tired after my first day of tree tagging. The afternoon has been productive on many levels. A feeling of peace fills me as I walk back to the van. My tool belt feels heavier now, and it's a relief to remove it to the back seat. My husband has been with my mom all afternoon. It's time to get back to them and call it a day.

Tomorrow will come.

The sun will rise, and it will be time to begin again.

Chapter 8

Pea

(Family Fabaceae)

Feeding the Soil

The Pea family is huge, comprising hundreds of genera and thousands of species—including trees! Many of these form fragrant, decorative flowers. Redbud, Texas ebony, and palo verde are beautiful examples. Redbud trees occur as both eastern and western species (but not in all states), while Texas ebony is native only to south Texas into the Chihuahuan Desert. Palo verde and mesquite are both keystone plants in their desert biome of the southern and southwestern United States into Mexico, with palo verde having the larger range. Trees in the Pea family are often armed with thorns, and they typically (not always) produce edible, seed-filled pods. Black locust (depicted above) offers edible flowers, but every other part is toxic including the seed pods. Water locust mostly inhabits east Texas into the southeastern states; its cousin, honey locust, has a smaller native range but is cultivated far beyond that across the entire continent. Kentucky coffeetree is found in the eastern two thirds of North America.

Day two of the tree labeling project arrives with the same beautiful weather as day one. In Minnesota, weather is the first thing one usually notices and shares as part of the morning routine. Still drowsy, I grab my gear and make my way over to the meeting place Susan Jane and I have settled on for this morning. I pull into Como Lakeside Pavilion parking lot, turn off the engine, and settle in to wait for her arrival. Knowing that 38 trees will all be labeled by the end of the day fills me with both incentive and enthusiasm. More than half of these are species we have added to the original self-guided map. Gratitude washes through me for being able to share my love of trees with people in this way. Not yet feeling quite awake, I sip from my water bottle, lean back in my seat, and close my still-sleepy eyes.

My mind drifts back again to the day of my first Tree Trek. It took place on a Saturday in late June. The day unfolded warmly, temperatures in the upper 70s with a low dew point. It was the kind of perfect summer day we dream of during winter. The night before, I had hardly slept out of sheer nervousness. Prepping extensively for an event like this helps tremendously, but that doesn't mean it calms anxiety or induces sleep. Having never led an outdoor talk before, I didn't know what to expect. My experience giving presentations to schools and library programs, however, where I share the art process of illustrating children's picture books did provide me with an invaluable foundation, not to be discounted. One thing often leads to another in life, even if you have no idea how or where that future will unfold!

When morning arrived at last, I felt much better getting ready, up and moving about. By the time I was dressed and pinning on my naturalist ID tag, I felt calm (enough) and full of glad anticipation. The moment for carrying on my dad's legacy had arrived! It was a reality. This thought lifted me considerably. Going over my detailed tree notes one more time, an unexpected image arose in my mind of all those trees in the park waiting for me. Looking up spontaneously, I spoke aloud a realization, as if hearing my dad's voice telling me, the way he would talk to me,

"You're among friends!"

Yes! I am. I feel support, energy, and love coming from trees, and this thought calmed me as I drove to the designated meeting place for Tree Trek. Two of my dad's ski friends showed up, a couple well-known to me. What a nice surprise! Then a very close friend of mine joined the group as well. I soon came to understand that everyone who had signed up for Tree Trek brought with them some sort of positive connection with trees, and therefore, was just as interested in being here as I was. The truth is, all sorts of friends surrounded me!

We started off beneath the honey locust tree (*Gleditsia triacanthos*). The leaves of this tree fluttered merrily above us, creating a delicate shade for us to gather beneath. Honey locust leaves are described in botany as pinnate. Another way to say it is they are pinnately compound. This type of leaf arrangement presents leaflets running along both sides of a central stalk (referred to as a "rachis" in botany), like a feather, making an almost lacelike effect. This is definitely not the verdantly deep shade of an American basswood, for example, with its large, simple leaves. On young, vigorous shoots, honey locust typically takes the pinnate concept further and outdoes itself by sending out twice-pinnate (bipinnate) leaves, very much like a fern. The tip of each honey locust leaf ends in two opposite leaflets on either side, with usually no leaflet coming out the center. In contrast, the pinnate leaves of black locust (*Robinia pseudoacacia*) typically send a single leaflet out the terminal end. Checking for a terminal leaflet is an especially useful way to distinguish between these two, say, for example, if locust sprouts appear in spring in the yard of the new house you just purchased. No flowers, no fruit, and both types of trees around in the neighborhood. How would you know? So there's one way to distinguish honey locust, which is edible, from its mostly toxic look-alike, black locust.

The fossil record shows that both tree species date back to the Pleistocene Epoch, the glacial period informally referred to as the "Great Ice Age." The park locusts are mostly thornless varieties, but originally, both honey locust and black locust trees had thorns up and down their branches and trunks, theorized to give protection against large bite-taking mastodons, giant sloths, and other megafauna of the Pleistocene.

Honey locust and black locust both belong to the Pea family, the same family in which all legumes are classified. Like other legumes such as beans or peas, many (not all) trees in the Pea family can enrich the soil they're growing in by "fixing" nitrogen. In a win-win relationship, bacteria on root nodules (or in the soil) do something the plant cannot; they convert nitrogen from the air into an organic form the tree needs in order to feed itself. They "fix" the nitrogen so the plant can use it. In return, the bacteria get carbohydrates (sugars) from the plant and a safe place to live.

What an amazing discovery it was to learn that a tree can also be a legume! Unlike a garden vegetable, however, black locust is toxic in all parts except for the lovely, white flowers which bloom about the same time as the honey locust flowers do. Black locust flowers have a subtle, indescribable taste all their own that you just have to experience; pick a few to try when the blossoms are still freshly crisp. Delectable! Black locust flowers are luscious, and exotic when sprinkled on salads or batter fried into little flower fritters. Again, the rest of the plant is potentially fatal to animals and humans. So, don't eat black locust pods or any other part of the tree.

Honey locust, on the other hand, is named for the sweet pulp lining the fully matured seed pods. As with any wild edible, some people are sensitive to it and may experience some unpleasant side effects. So, proceed at your own risk, slowly and with caution. For millennia, however, humans have survived by wild foraging the bounty nature provides around us, including scraping out the sweet pulp of honey locust pods. Also edible are the young pods when they are unripe and tender. As for the honey locust flowers, well, just don't eat those!

Come fall, distinguishing between these two trees is very easy by observing their fruit. Black locust pods are only about three to four inches long, straight, brownish tan at maturity and thin. Honey locust pods at maturity, on the other hand, are a deep, rich, brownish-purple color and hang in long, wide twists up to 15 inches long. Telling them apart by comparing leaflet shape is a bit trickier, both being roundish with no pointed tip. Still, if you look closely, honey locust leaflets are more oval compared with those of the round-shaped black locust, and very much smaller. In addition, black locust leaves are always pinnate, never twice pinnate like honey locust.

Black locust's native origins are in the Ozark and Appalachian regions, but it was historically planted all across North America (and Europe) for its hard, rot-resistant wood, the prized acacia honey made from its flowers, and its ability to withstand erosion. Outside its native range, black locust has over time become considered invasive in many regions because of its aggressive habit of spreading by root suckering and crowding out native species. While mowing happens routinely beneath our park's tagged tree, in the wilder, uncultivated areas, black locust is proliferating quite well. Honey locust, on the other hand, is nontoxic, grows taller, and has male, thornless cultivars—all good reasons why this tree is a great choice for lining the streets of the park or introducing into a yard. Come autumn, honey locust's dainty yellow leaves carpet the area beneath each canopy, creating an engaging musical swish-through experience a bit different from the ruffle-through sounds of most deciduous leaves. Drums vs. the triangle in the percussion section is my analogy for that contrast—a bit of whimsy to end with.

And that covered the honey locust.

For my next stop on that first Tree Trek, I led the way up the nearby gentle slope and gestured toward the top where the trees native to the Rocky Mountains and westward grow. "Does it feel a bit cooler to you now?" I joked as we climbed. "We're heading up into the mountains!"

A woman traversing the grass next to me made friendly conversation along the way, memorable afterward because she introduced herself as Susan Jane.

"I worked with your dad on the Environment Committee, and I remember your daughter attended at least one of his early Tree Treks."

"Really? She never told me that!"

Another surprise revelation! I've since learned from my daughter, Sonia, that Grandpa took her on many such adventure walks and rambles through the park. She's a geologist now and has enriched the expansion project by computer generating a printable map showing all the new, tagged tree locations. She has her own memories and tree stories that hold roots of meaning for her reaching way back. In fact, she told me later, "Grandpa and I talked a lot about trees. I loved those times with him. Grandpa showed me what buckthorn was, and honey locust. I always thought 'locust' was a funny name for a tree!"

My thought exactly!

At the top of the "Rocky Mountains" hill, the group settled in beneath the Douglas-fir, and I went through my remarks outlined for that tree. Continuing on my planned route, we made stops at white fir and the ponderosa grove. Crossing from there past the labyrinth to what I call the Ohio Buckeye Valley, we made a quick stop at the ironwood tree and the northern catalpa growing right next to each other. Susan Jane asked good questions or made relevant comments at many of these stops. She seemed very interested and knowledgeable, and this impressed me.

Still sitting and resting in the car, my thoughts land pleasantly upon each of these trees to which I led people on that first Tree Trek, and they soon branch into a myriad of connections, like roots and synapses sparking memories, conversations, and interactions unrolling in a list of experiences that nourish and enrich my life.

The lovely, white flowers of the northern catalpa (*Catalpa speciosa*) blanket its branches in June. This is a hardy species in the tropical Trumpet Creeper family (Bignoniaceae), growing very well in temperate regions. The petals present their own, purple-speckled landing pad complete with two, fuzzy yellow beacons guiding the way in for arriving pollinators. My dad shared with me his enthusiasm over discovering their gorgeous flowers in the park, sending me a photo which I now use as a reference. In the fall, the 10 to 20-inch-long, cigar-like, slender pods hang down in a vivid exhibition of catalpa's method for producing seeds.

The pretty nutlet clusters of the ironwood tree (*Ostrya virginiana*) decoratively ornament this understory shrub of the upland forests (sugar maple-basswood), a sight that fills me with gladness. It reminds me of the oaks, evergreens, ferns, and wildflowers that grow alongside them, and how the nutlets sustain squirrels, mice, and a huge variety of birds. In winter, ironwood's amber-colored leaves remain on their delicate twigs until spring, brightening the otherwise bare, dark trunks of other tree species growing alongside it.

An Ohio buckeye (*Aesculus glabra*) grew in the yard when we bought our house, my first introduction (having never seen or noticed one until then). My dad became very interested in my identification of this tree, for it was new to him as well. The leaves of this tree grow in an arrangement called palmately compound, where several leaflets making up the leaf radiate outwardly from a central point, like fingers from the palm of your hand. Even though its seeds bear some resemblance to a chestnut with their glossy brown color and eyespot, they're neither closely related nor even a true nut; Ohio buckeye fruit is a capsule that splits open to reveal one to three seeds inside and is basically toxic to humans (unless properly prepared). People sometimes carry an Ohio buckeye seed in their pocket for good luck. Horse chestnut (*Aesculus hippocastanum*), the buckeye's European cousin, is not really a chestnut (or a true nut) either—both trees belonging to the Soapberry family (Sapindaceae). Our large buckeye tree broke in half after a summer windstorm one year, crashing over the neighbor's driveway. We left the stump there, now an attractive shrub of buckeye suckers continuing to provide a living screen from the neighboring yard, and gloriously alive in springtime with buzzing bees pollinating their flower clusters. Every one of those seeds formed from the flowers a squirrel will claim, bury, eat, and otherwise make off with, for they love those "nuts!" In winter, buckeye leaf scars beam out smiles, each face with a slightly different expression and variation especially on younger sprouts with their particularly large buds topping the faces like a hat. The portrait gallery of photos I made one year consists entirely of buckeye leaf-scar "faces."

At these recollections, I take a deep breath and breathe out a happy sigh as a feeling of joy washes through me.

Research studies have shown that walking among or just living near trees can benefit human health. In Japan, a meditative walk through a forest heals in the way known as *shinrin-yoku,* translating as "forest bathing." Forest researchers also have uncovered a vast social network shared among trees which includes hormonal, electrical signals, warnings of danger, shared nutrients, and more. Depending on the species, important, symbiotic relationships develop into a vast, complex network between tree roots and the fungi that grow within or on them. Trees communicate. People have assumed that trees compete in an ongoing battle for nutrients, light, and water, with the winner beating out the others in a battle of survival of the fittest, leaving the loser in the shade to wither and die. Some researchers are beginning to question such generalizing assumptions. The relationships within a mature forest are much more complex. Two trees planted or happening to grow right next to each other are not necessarily competing for resources, energy, sunlight, air space, or growth. Scientists are now providing evidence that trees are communal, cooperative, and interdependent.

Most of a tree's roots grow less than 12 inches or so below the soil surface. In deeper soils, many trees will drop some sinker roots which serve to stabilize the tree, but the vast majority of fine roots stay shallow and spread away from the trunk, two to three times the canopy's radius. Quite a distance! All those roots are busy. Nitrogen fixation among legumes is only one way to bring in more nutrients, and that ability is limited to only some tree species. Most trees on earth, in general, use a remarkable method to further increase their water and nutrient uptake in a process that involves fungi living in the soil around their roots. This association between a root and a fungus working together to benefit both organisms through symbiosis is called a mycorrhiza. My dad's career in plant pathology, starting in the 1960s, involved researching (and teaching) the physiology and interactions of host-parasite relationships of fungi. His work concentrated not on mycorrhizal symbiosis, but rather on parasitism in the newly burgeoning field of modern mycotoxicology to which he contributed much.

There are so many paths one can take, so many aspects one can cover when talking about trees!

The purr of a car pulling into the parking lot, and then a door shutting, brings me out of my reverie. I open my eyes to find Susan Jane making her way over to my van. I get out and, on second thought, pull open the sliding door and invite her to sit down for a while. Instead of just setting right off, I feel like talking, getting to know her a bit. She joins me in the open space of the side door.

"I didn't sleep well last night," I tell her, yawning and stretching. "In fact, I haven't slept well for some time now!"

"Oh, I've been through that before. I feel for you," she replies.

"Yes, I'm caregiving for my mother this week with the help of my husband. He joined me this time so he could keep her company while I do this project."

"That's so helpful," says Susan Jane. "Be sure to thank him for me!"

For the next several minutes or so we plant the little garden of a new friendship, feeding it with our empathic talk. We talk about our mothers, our family dynamics and difficulties that formed our growth as children. What our adult sibling relationships are like now. What our dads were like.

"My dad had to have things his way," I say.

"My dad was an absolute perfectionist!" she replies.

It feels good knowing that we all arrive from different paths. Each childhood is filled with circumstances and contexts that include the joy of roses and sunshine, but not exclusively that. Many things shape us both good and bad; all of us are fragile beings, searching, doing our best in living our lives to flourish, grow, and find happiness. We all need each other.

The morning is moving on, though, and Kentucky coffeetree awaits. "We should get going," I say.

We hitch up our totes and gear, and set off to tag another leguminous tree in the Pea family, Kentucky coffeetree (*Gymnocladus dioicus*), named by English speakers for its dark brown, shiny seeds these early settlers used as a coffee substitute until the real thing became more widely available. One problem (besides the bitter taste) is that at least three hours of roasting is required to neutralize the toxic alkaloids. Like the locust trees, these trees also date back to the Pleistocene. Though toxic to modern-day creatures (who simply avoid them), the seed pods were desirable food for the now extinct megafauna of that time with the capacity to chew through their thick walls, deal with the hard seeds, and get after the sweet, gooey pulp surrounding them. Without those ancient mammals to scarify the extremely hard seed coatings and allow the seeds to take up water and germinate, Kentucky coffeetree has difficulty propagating naturally by seed. This means most Kentucky coffeetrees in the wild expand themselves through root suckering. The problem here is that this leads to a monoclonal culture made up of just a few individuals and a limited gene pool. Luckily, the assets of attractiveness, hardiness, and disease resistance do have benefits, for horticulturists continue to cultivate coffeetree seedlings in nurseries for planting on urban boulevards. Think about adding this tree if you have a place to plant one!

The Kentucky coffeetree we're headed for lives just off the lower walking path under the pedestrian bridge. At first glance, you might mistake its pinnate leaves as belonging to honey locust, especially since they are also twice pinnate. But our coffeetree's leaflets are longer and larger with a little pointed tip on the end instead of rounded, which helps with identification. Also, *all* the leaves on a Kentucky coffeetree are bipinnately compound (again, like a fern), not just the tips of branches as in honey locust. Knowing this, the other differences become clearer, such as a significantly larger leaf size (up to three feet!) and vastly different fruit.

The coffeetree we're about to retag is a male who's lost his sign. We'll get more into gender later. For now, let's simply say his mate is on our list as one of the new tagged trees because I want to draw people's attention to the female Kentucky coffeetree's attractive seed pods. Wide, flat, and leathery, they deserve the attention. Deep purplish brown when mature, the large pods feel good in the palm of your hand. Even after all the leaves have dropped in autumn, the pods remain decoratively hanging on the branches through winter. Our female tree lives on the other side of the pedestrian bridge beyond the Avenue of the Giants (as I call it), just up the hill from those huge specimens that date back to some of the original trees planted over 100 years ago. They are absolutely magnificent. She is a much smaller, younger tree and is resplendently clad with clusters of gorgeous pods.

By now, Susan Jane and I have an easy pattern of approaching a tree and finding the best place to pound in its sign. After our recent, intense conversation sharing confidences, a burst of silliness comes over me. In front of the Kentucky coffeetree, I jokingly undulate my arms up and down as if to capture the tree's vibrations or emanations.

"Feel the energy," I intone with closed eyes. "The tree will lead us to just the right spot."

And it does. We laugh as we locate that place in a moment of shared camaraderie.

"It truly does take some evaluation," she says.

She's right, and every place we pick out together feels absolutely right.

"It's nice to have someone to do this with," I say, adding with a wink, "especially someone from the Committee."

"Of course," she smiles in return, emanating an energy of her own into the lightness that has grown between us, one that feels just like the best part of what I receive from trees.

Chapter 9
Poplar
(Genus *Populus*)

Finding Meaning in Names

Aspens, poplars, and cottonwoods share the Populus genus in the Willow family. Plains, southern, and Rio Grande cottonwoods are subspecies of eastern cottonwood (Populus deltoides), *all being massive and resplendent trees of floodplain areas across much of North America. Swamp cottonwood* (Populus heterophylla) *stays in areas too wet even for eastern cottonwood. In the western areas of the continent grow narrowleaf cottonwood* (Populus augustifolia) *and black cottonwood* (Populus trichocarpa). *Fremont cottonwood* (Populus fremontii) *stays in the Southwest, with Mexican cottonwood* (Populus mexicana) *further south. Balsam poplar* (Populus balsamifera) *is a cold-loving tree of the north extending into the boreal zone. Bigtooth aspen* (Populus grandidentata), *a mostly upland forest tree, stays in the eastern half of the continent into Canada and is often a neighbor of quaking aspen* (Populus tremuloides), *though the latter has a much wider distribution. Populus species can hybridize when growing near each other, such as with white poplar* (Populus alba), *an introduced species from Europe.*

What's in a name? A lot! Their cultural and historical meanings can vary so much and describe things so differently across diverse cultures. While European settlers were roasting and grinding Kentucky coffeetree seeds to remind them of home as they moved west, Indigenous Peoples had less need for a poor approximation of that beverage. Although the Meskwaki Nation are noted to consume the seeds for a hot beverage, most Indigenous Peoples' traditions involve using the seeds and other parts differently. The pulverized root bark held widespread use as an effective treatment for constipation across native cultures, and the seeds were universally enjoyed as counters in gambling. Given these uses, the various names tribal nations have for this tree may be just as colorful as what Kentucky land speculators enticing settlers "west" began calling it long ago.

Sometimes, on the other hand, names coalesce across cultures. American basswood's name comes from the word "bast," referring to the fibrous inner bark which Indigenous Peoples across North America put to extensive use for making cord and rope and were doing so when early settlers arrived on the scene. In the Ojibwe language, bast is called *wiigob*, the same name for the basswood tree itself. The processed bast fiber is called *asigobaan*, indicative of the extensive use of this product and therefore the need to name it. Some colonists were well aware of bast and had used the inner bark for the same purpose historically back in their native homelands. Some newcomers dubbed this New World tree for its important use as bast, which morphed into the word "basswood." Others, recognizing the strong similarity of American basswood to their own European native *Tilia* species, called this New World tree American linden. In German, "linden" translates as *linde*, in Norwegian and Swedish, *lind*. The "Father of Taxonomy" himself, Swedish botanist Carl Linnaeus, got his surname from his father who was required to take a permanent surname upon entering the University of Lund in the late 1600s. His father chose a latinized version of the word "linden," based on a huge, old linden tree growing in the local area of his childhood home.

Trees of the poplar genus (*Populus*) generally refer to aspens, poplars, and cottonwoods; they are classified alongside trees of the willow genus (*Salix*) into the Willow family. Often, common names of trees in the *Populus* genus are used interchangeably; for example, black cottonwood is also known as the western balsam poplar. Aspens began to be colloquially referred to (regardless of species) in some regions of the United States as "popple," including in Minnesota. Most likely, this is because the German word for poplar is *pappel*, and in Swedish, *poppel*, reflecting the ethnicity of some states' early white settlers. In the 1700s, colonists brought along with them their favorite trees including introducing a new tree to North America, white poplar (*Populus alba*), mostly because it is so attractive with the leaf's white-toned, furry underside which stands out so prettily in contrast to the leaf top's dark green.

Like black locust, however, white poplar has become considered an invasive species in many regions and threatens to overtake native landscapes with its root-suckering habit of spreading.

About 30 species of *Populus* grow around the world. Trees in this genus share one very striking characteristic. Their leaf stalks, or petioles, are flattened, presenting a little sideways sail for each leaf that causes them to tremble and flutter in the slightest puff of breeze. This is how Carl Linnaeus came up with their genus name. In Latin, *populus* means "people," and to Linnaeus the continual rustling of poplar leaves sounded like a crowd of murmuring voices. This, I can attest to with confidence, works for any culture! What all these voices are saying and in what language offers up an interesting compilation of tree stories that describe a time, a place, and a people.

Susan Jane and I now make our way back toward the Lakeside Pavilion parking lot, having finished with the Kentucky coffeetree area. Our plan is to cover ground along the lakeshore and then head to the trees located by the Historic Streetcar Station (a city landmark now repurposed as the District 10 park office). That is my hope, anyway. Given the time allotted, the goal for the day all at once feels both overwhelming and yet still possible to attain. I take a breath and decide to just enjoy things, and not worry about what doesn't get completed. Walking companionably, the two of us are contemplative for a moment, just looking around and enjoying the day. Rounding the curve of the pedestrian path, we exit the shade of the evergreens to step into the sunlight of the open parking lot where the alternately fluttering green and white leaves of white poplar catch our attention. They are waving resplendently from their magnificent trees, beautifully reminding me that they are next in line for our work today.

Shortly after my dad died, I was looking over his bookshelf when my eye fell upon a small tree ID book. My hands immediately reached over to pull it out. Flipping through, I found a leaf pressed between the pages where the book easily opened. The "leaf" was actually one leaflet taken from the palmately compound leaf of an Ohio buckeye, and it was pressed between the buckeye pages (of course!). Surprised, I let this sight soak through me for a while, pleased to have found an artifact my dad had placed here. It reminded me of his interest long ago in our yard's buckeye tree I had identified for him.

Perhaps it was even from that one! My heart warmed at this thought. Toward the back of the book, a small, white piece of paper appeared on which he had written a short list. It reads:

Starting at Pavilion
White Poplar
Black Willow
American Elm
Crabapple, ornamental
Green Ash
River Birch

When it came time to bump up the map of tagged trees, this list struck me as essential to include. The row of trees it refers to grow along the lakeshore and represent species he felt were important enough to note. In addition, I surmised that other people on the walking path were like me, who, many years even before my naturalist proclivities kicked in, might want to know the name that belongs to the attractive leaves of what I now know to be white poplar. Green ash is the only tree on the list that is gone now, destroyed by the emerald ash borer invasion. We have no tag for green ash because the city foresters have removed all those trees from the park. Locating the rest of the list, however, was meaningful to me. It connected me to my dad's thought process besides giving me species he'd already identified in the area I could use to educate myself. From the list, I learned to identify white poplar, black willow, and river birch and the general areas in the park where they grow.

Of all the trees on the list, black willow (*Salix nigra*) proved to be the most difficult to find, requiring me to study up on willows. In the process, the first and easiest fact I learned was that willows are classified in the Willow family. Thank you very much! I learned that black willow is native to North America. Nice! I also learned that the *Salix* genus of willows is made up of over 400 species of trees and shrubs worldwide, with around 100 species native to North America. Wow! This, in contrast to the mere 30 or so comprising the *Populus* genus worldwide, with only eight of those species native to North America.

All trees (and plants in general) can hybridize in nature on their own, sometimes even evolving into new species; more often they appear as varieties adapted to new environments with the added benefit of inserting genetic diversity back into an existing species. With willows, however, things can get a bit complicated. Willows often and easily hybridize, which can make it hard to tell species apart. It's just the way willows are. They also easily propagate, not just from seed dispersal but through cloning of their twigs. Twigs break off and readily take root either where they land or after floating downstream in their watery habitats. Of the willows settlers from overseas introduced as nonnatives, at least three are now naturalized on this continent. One European variety brought by homesteaders moving west, the whitecrack willow, was already hybridized in Europe before arriving here where it tends to crowd out native species. Despite (or perhaps because of) this, willows in general seem very well adapted. Their highly variable nature allows them to pioneer ever-changing landscapes—their strategy to survive to where they are today in willow evolution. Their story.

When I was 12, my dad gave me *Wind in the Willows*. I absolutely loved Kenneth Grahame's classic children's book (and still do), letting the full color illustrations inspire my imagination and draw me into its world. My favorite line from one of the color illustration plates always comes to mind when I think of that book. In that scene, Mole is greatly excited to be out on the river for the first time (having never even seen a river before) with his new friend, Rat, who has invited him on a picnic excursion in his boat.

"Please! Ratty, *I* want to row!"

Grahame's story takes place in Great Britain, and the trees he's referring to are probably weeping willows (*Salix babylonica*) growing on the banks of a fictional river, probably inspired by the River Thames in southern England where Grahame spent much of his childhood. Like him, I was lucky enough to grow up near a weeping willow in my own neighborhood. As children we used to pretend we were in the jungle and swing from the drooping branches. The brittle branches often broke, but we didn't care. I wouldn't trade those memories for anything!

Starting at Pavilion.

When I was first scoping things out for our work today, white poplar was easy to locate. Black willow, second on the list, was more elusive. I had learned it prefers moist soils, a good reason why it was on my dad's list for this pedestrian path area along the lakeshore. Many willows, I had also learned, have a very pale underside to their leaves in contrast to deeper green leaf tops; black willow, on the other hand, presents both sides of its leaves as pretty much the same shade of green—one very good way to ID them. A huge willow grows right next to the pavilion, but its leaves show light yellow green on the underside, so I quickly dismissed that one. After bushwhacking along the somewhat overgrown lakeshore to get up close to the willow trees there, I gave up. While my first attempt to scout out black willow ended in failure, I did make the connection to the sucker sprouts my dad and I planted lakeside to the family cabin in northern Minnesota back when I was a teenager. Out of all the suckers we planted those many decades ago, only one survived. That one I now know is a black willow, and it truly is a survivor. Many years earlier, beavers had chewed about halfway through the trunk, then stopped, leaving a big gap. The tree had gone on through the decades growing around the gap leaving a big scar as the only reminder of beaver activities while it recovered and flourished. Today that black willow has grown into a 14-inch-diameter beauty.

As Susan Jane and I approach the two white poplars growing by the lake, I show her which one I think will work best. A small path through the underbrush and grasses leads to each, but one of the white poplars is more visible from the pedestrian path than the other. We think a tag on that more visible one will entice people in, and together we settle on a suitably flat spot. As usual, I proceed to pound in the nails. I explain how I've spent some time on previous visits searching for the black willow and have not been successful in finding it, at least not yet.

"We're running short on time," I continue. "Let's leave black willow for later and head toward the Streetcar Station trees."

"Sure, that sounds good. Do you think you'll even find the black willow?" Susan Jane asks.

"I definitely will," I reply. "I'll return later today or tomorrow and keep searching until I find it."

She knows neither the backstory of the list nor of my determination to find the tree species on it. I plan to locate the black willow later this week and wire the ID sign onto what I'm pretty confident will be a clump of smallish trunks. Black willow is not an especially tall tree, though it can attain a 20-inch diameter. Based on my false starts so far, I expect it will take more bushwhacking through the underbrush than I had bargained for. I also know that in my gear and hiking boots I contrast starkly with the dress and demeanor of the urban walkers streaming past me just a few feet away on the paved path. Like before, I will once again studiously ignore them as I know they are studiously ignoring me in return. The urban way to get along after all!

So, having decided black willow can wait a bit, we stroll onward past the maple trees tagged from yesterday, enjoying along the way the verdant green and deep shade cascading from deciduous trees and evergreens alike.

With the many and varied common names in use for trees, Carl Linnaeus's taxonomic-nomenclature system of using two latinized names (genus and species) plays an important role in making sure two people are talking about the same thing. The Linnaean system of scientific classification is important, also, as an international language for sharing information, as common names in different languages can be both incomprehensible and unpronounceable. Using the *Genus/species* name provides unambiguous, familiar identifiers with which to successfully communicate. Formal, latinized nomenclature provides a key to the map leading out of the labyrinths and rabbit holes into which common names can lead us.

Blue beech, ironwood, and American beech are perfect examples of this.

Blue beech (*Carpinus caroliniana*) is a very touchable tree with thin, gray bark that all but invites hands to run along its surface, which is smooth and sinewy. For this reason, it is also called musclewood. Blue beech is also known as American hornbeam due to the extreme hardness of its wood and a fine grain that polishes up to resemble a horn. *Beam* means "tree" in Old English. Here's where things get tangled. Blue beech is also sometimes called ironwood (the tree we met in the previous chapter), again, because of its very hard wood. Ironwood (*Ostrya virginiana*), on the other hand, is also known as American hop hornbeam. The additional "hop" is due to the fact that its nutlets resemble those of hops, and the "hornbeam" because, again, it is also a very hard wood. If this isn't confusing enough, I should mention that blue beech is NOT in the Beech family (*Fagaceae*) at all! At this point, it may come as a relief to know that both blue beech and ironwood, while not in the same genus, are at least classified into the same family, the Birch family of Betulaceae. Like all birches, these two species have catkins, dangling spikes of tightly clustered male or female flowers. Their leaves are similar as well, and both sexes of catkins occur on the same tree. Better yet, a very easy way exists for telling the difference between the two species. Simply observe the smooth, sensual bark of the blue beech as opposed to the roughly textured, vertically rectangular plates of the ironwood. Again, these two trees, with all their common name similarities and their Birch family classification, still belong to separate genera.

To further confound things, American beech (*Fagus grandifolia*) is often confused with blue beech. This mix up is due to a slight similarity between the leaves, and to a much greater extent because of their shared quality of smooth, gray bark. Both tree trunks are similarly inviting to touch. American beech, however, produces true nuts, and is classified in the Fagaceae family along with oaks and chestnuts. Besides the fact that American beech is a much larger tree (up to 70′ tall with a trunk diameter than can get to 3′ across) in contrast to blue beech, an understory tree, a very easy way to distinguish between the two species is to compare their winter twigs when there are no leaves to get in the way. The narrow buds of an American beech are so long (up to 3/4″) and so widely angled away from the twig that they almost resemble thorns. Once you know what to look for, you can also locate these buds in summer. No matter the season, making the ID this way is unmistakable.

Arriving at the Historic Streetcar Station, Susan Jane and I head straight for the American beech tree. I greet the tree. "Hi there, American beech! Ready for your sign?"

It smiles back at us in the midday sunshine, perhaps not flexing its muscles quite like a blue beech does, but its comparatively smooth bark comes pretty close.

"Susan Jane," I say directly, "I can't mar this beautiful bark by putting a sign on it right in front."

"Yes, I agree," she replies calmly, "we should put it on the side or back."

"Let's do the swamp white oak first," I suggest, needing a little time in preparation for pounding nails into this tree. Swamp white oak is only about 15 feet away and is easily dispatched, forcing us to retrace our steps back to the American beech again. The extra time, however, seems to have solidified things for us. We walk around the tree once more, but we both already know the sign should face toward the nearby swamp white oak sign we've just attached.

"They can talk to each other!" we both say almost simultaneously, then laugh together at our silliness.

Nails bend once again as the very dense wood of American beech resists my efforts, but it accepts the situation in the end.

Our tagged eastern redcedar (*Juniperus virginiana*) grows in the same area as the American beech but is much more visible alongside the street and walking trail. An abundant grove thrives there, and the chosen tree shines from all directions. That is why I chose her, because she's in the prime of life, adorned with an array of gorgeous, blue, ripening cones. I refer to her as "she" because eastern redcedar is an example of a plant species whose male and female reproductive parts appear on separate trees. The male trees produce pollen cones that appear much different from the seed cones of the female. Her cones look like small blue berries, but they are not berries at all. In the grocery store, however, they are referred to as "juniper berries." Small mammals thrive on her "fruit," as do several bird species who also use the thick foliage for nesting and roosting. Edibility of eastern redcedar seed cones for humans goes back hundreds of generations. The Lakota use them to flavor meats such as for stewing with venison. Distillers also use them in the production of gin—again, as a flavoring. Harvest the berry-like cones when they're blue and fully mature, from late fall into winter or even spring, and you'll have an interesting culinary seasoning to add to your spice rack. A tea made of the leaves provides a flavorful beverage high in vitamin C.

Eastern redcedar also offers another example of common names confusing things. Just like our friend northern white cedar, eastern redcedar is not a true cedar either. The genus name, *Juniperus*, tells us that this tree is actually a juniper. I suspect the reason *Juniperus* continues to be most commonly referred to as a "cedar" is because of its cedar-like aroma. I still have an eastern redcedar log my dad gave me that he found years ago in the park. The tree had fallen, and he'd cut a few logs to take home with him to burn in the fireplace for their pleasant fragrance. He always knew how much I love wood and respected my creative use of saws, drills, and hammers.

"Maybe you could cut these into coasters," he said those many years ago, handing me a rough log, "or to use as aromatic pieces you could put in a drawer. Take it home and see what you can do with it."

"Thanks, Dad."

Here I am, decades later, "doing something with it." Besides sawing off a few slices for myself over the years, I'm now learning so much about trees and sharing so many aspects of that knowledge with others. I didn't know it at the time, but my science professor dad, who loved to teach and encourage others, had already begun sharing his wonderful legacy with me.

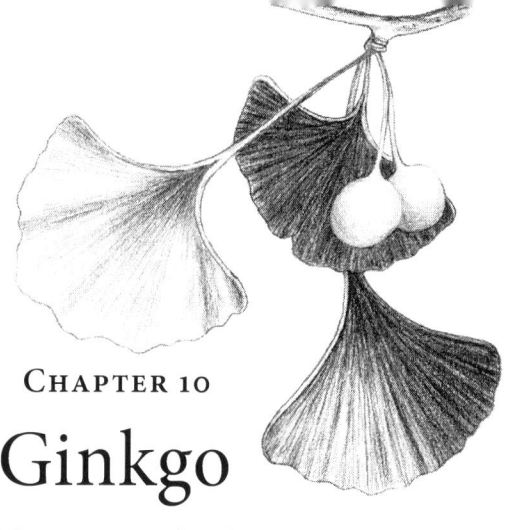

Chapter 10
Ginkgo
(Genus *Ginkgo*)
Millennia of Life Renewing

Arising over 200 million years ago, the lineage of Ginkgo biloba *dates back as one of Earth's most ancient seed-bearing trees. Leaf fossils reveal that several genera and many species of ginkgo trees were once widespread across the planet on every continent. During the Pleistocene ice age, regional populations of ginkgo began shrinking and eventually only one lone species remained—our* Ginkgo biloba *of today. About 1,000 years ago, people discovered ginkgos (most likely rare at the time) growing in their native homeland of south-central and eastern China. They soon came to revere the trees both for their beauty and edible seeds. Cultivation and nurturing over the centuries ensured this beloved species would persist and expand its reach. Today, the dainty, fan-shaped leaves of ginkgo trees decorate urban streets of modern cities worldwide. The International Union for Conservation of Nature (IUCN) Red List designates* Ginkgo biloba *as Endangered, however, due to its high risk of extinction in the wild populations that may remain.*

As Dutch elm disease unwound its unstoppable decimation, city foresters began to slowly replace the fallen giants. No longer did great, graceful limbs reach toward one another from across neighborhood streets to create shady archways as they once had for my own growing limbs to walk or bicycle beneath as a child. Just as with the emerald ash borer epidemic decades later, foresters sought replacements for the destroyed elms, including new cultivars resistant to Dutch elm disease. These new kids on the block brought with them hardy dispositions with combinations of pest, salt, and sulfur resistance, and a touch of drought tolerance thrown in for good measure.

Subsequently, the boulevard across from my parents' house acquired several such newcomers along its length. Maples, northern catalpas, honey locusts, Kentucky coffeetrees, and ginkgos began to appear in well-chosen variety packs around the city. When my dad discovered two ginkgos planted on the parkway boulevard right in front of their house, he was overjoyed. My enthusiasm for ginkgos arose, most likely, from his enthusiasm rubbing off on me—besides the fact that they are truly fascinating. My daughter says the same thing when describing his animated introduction to her of the two ginkgos on the parkway and explaining all about them. "I was amazed," she told me, "to learn from Grandpa that trees can be separately male and female, just like people!"

Frankly, I was equally astonished when I learned this as an adult! Many trees greet us as either male or female, such as ash, willow, juniper, and mulberry (to name a few). In botany, trees such as these with male and female reproductive parts occurring on separate individuals are known as dioecious (from Latin, "two houses"). Other trees do things the monoecious way (from Latin, meaning "one house") such as oaks, pines, and birches with their female and male parts located on the same tree. Things get trickier from here, though. Hermaphrodite trees, such as linden, apple, hackberry, and elm, have both male and female parts (stamen *and* pistil) present in the same flower, called bisexual or perfect flowers. Taking this further, both unisexual and bisexual flowers can be present in combinations on some monoecious trees, and sometimes within the same flower cluster, such as with the Ohio buckeye, where the upper flowers are primarily staminate (male), and the lower flowers are primarily perfect (both male and female). Then there is gender swapping, further blurring things in the tree world. For example, the striped maple (*Acer pensylvanicum*) changes sex repeatedly, sometimes year to year depending on various factors such as age, health, and environmental conditions.

Ginkgo is dioecious. Separate male and female trees rely on wind to pollinate between them in the spring. Male catkin-like cones release multitudes of pollen grains in the spring. Female ovules (the undeveloped seeds) hang open to the air, ready for pollination by producing a pollination droplet on each tip specifically made for drawing in a male gametophyte to start the long fertilization process. But wait! All this is actually conifer-like behavior! Yes, on first glance, ginkgo resembles any other deciduous tree with new leaves emerging in the spring and colorful fall foliage shedding in autumn, but that is where the resemblance ends.

Most deciduous trees are angiosperms, meaning they have proper flowers producing seeds within a protective ovary. Ginkgo trees do not have flowers. Ginkgo lineage goes back millions of years before any flowering trees appeared on the scene, to an ancient landscape that included conifers, cycads, and gnetophytes. These first seed-bearing trees are categorized as gymnosperms (literally, naked seed) because their ovules hang open to the air for pollination, not protected within flowers. Even ginkgo's vascular system within the inner wood resembles that of conifers, adding to the seemingly contradictory but useful, general description of ginkgo as a deciduous conifer. That said, ginkgos are not strictly conifers, although closely related. The first seed plants that remain from that prehistoric time comprise five separate groups: conifers, cycads, ginkgo, gnetophytes, and the flowering plants (angiosperms). The first four on that list are gymnosperms, and ginkgo is definitely one of those.

So, what exactly is going on in the deeper ginkgo world? Clearly, it's a lot more than meets the eye! One very dramatic trait that sets ginkgo apart from both deciduous trees *and* conifers, is the ginkgo pollen grain's germination of swimming sperm. In seed-bearing trees, this feature is shared only with the cycads. This trait dates even farther back to Earth's oldest lineages of seedless plants whose ancestors first evolved in water—ancient plants that include the ferns, mosses, algae, and horsetails.

Ginkgo biloba is often referred to as a "living fossil" because in comparing fossils to their counterparts in modern ginkgos, essentially no structural change has occurred. Just as they always have done for over the last 200 million years, ginkgo leaf veins fork into a Y pattern by twos from a common point fanning out with no main vein connecting them (called open dichotomous venation). This open veining system is relatively primitive compared with the way deciduous leaves formed in subsequent periods, and no other temperate, woody plant shares this. I'm glad! I love watching those charmingly distinctive leaves flutter daintily along the branches like little hands waving, or butterfly wings, or fans.

Ginkgo leaves have another distinctive trait in that they take two forms. Leaves that emerge in spring from the short, spur-like shoots running along the branches are more intact. Leaves that emerge later in the season on long shoots have an indent in the center of the fan creating two lobes; this is where the *biloba* species name derives. Even the way ginkgos go about dropping their leaves in autumn is unique. Instead of letting go of a few leaves at a time over days like other deciduous trees, ginkgo drops its brilliant yellow leaves all at once over hours or overnight.

Researchers studying the fossil record have determined that many species of *Ginkgo* began to die out during the Pleistocene ice age, most likely due to the colder, drier climate restricting their once widespread range. At the end of the last glaciation, ginkgos did not bounce back, perhaps also due to the loss of creatures that once dispersed their seed. For whatever reasons, our *Ginkgo biloba* of today retreated from a rather wide range throughout what is now Asia to rare and remnant forest enclaves in their native areas of what is now south-central and eastern China, where they currently persevere in the wild. Ginkgo's continued survival was further ensured through cultivation, first in China about 1,000 years ago, then through trade routes from China into Korea and Japan around the 13th or 14th century. Lovingly expanding on this, Japanese horticulturists carefully transplanted ginkgos across their nation. Like the revered linden or lime trees of Europe, ginkgos become beloved it seems wherever they are gifted, grown, or transplanted, and are now enjoyed in urban streetscapes across the world—including my dad's boulevard across the street where they invoke delight in any language.

The *Ginkgo biloba* we are lucky enough to have with us today is the sole surviving species from a diverse ginkgo lineage that once lived on every continent across the planet. It appears *Ginkgo biloba* got pretty lucky, too!

One remarkable trait contributing to ginkgo's hardiness is its robust immune system. Individuals can easily live 1,000 years and more, especially when protected in such areas as temple gardens over centuries, and as long as they are growing in the temperate climate they love with the right moisture conditions. In addition to their strong immunity, ginkgos have insect-resistant leaves, are cold tolerant, and are able to withstand harsh urban conditions.

Ginkgo also has a stocked toolbox of reproductive survival strategies that have contributed to its seemingly unstoppable resilience. Peter Crane's marvelous book, *Ginkgo: The Tree that Time Forgot*, describes one of the more sensational tools ginkgo possesses as embedded buds hidden within the axils of each leaf. These buds gradually become buried in the wood of the growing tree, but are potentially always at the ready to kick in and emerge when faced with complete devastation, such as a tree losing all its limbs. Some very old ginkgos can produce downward growth from these hidden buds to ground level, growing new trunks, branches, and roots, essentially ensuring that the ginkgo tree reproduces itself. New growth can also sprout downward from the buds that remain from the very first leaves the ginkgo tree formed as a seedling, buried deep within the tree's base. These can sometimes form surface roots called lignotubers, anchoring a new shoot to the soil.

Juxtaposed against such seeming immortality, I feel grateful for the companionship ginkgos offer as peaceful ambassadors of renewal and ongoing life. Ginkgos endure, perhaps not quite so timelessly as the light, air, and water that feed them, but they do give the effect of coming pretty close!

When Susan Jane and I arrive at the ginkgo grove, I show her the large male I would like to tag. It overlooks the street and is not near any walking path, but it does lead to other tagged trees in a coherent sequence for the walking tour.

"Yes, this is a beauty," she agrees, reading the sign before giving it to me to attach. "I see that 'cone', 'conifer', and 'deciduous' are all used in the text for this. Interesting…because deciduous trees don't have cones, right?"

"Right," I reply, "except for ginkgos! Male ginkgos produce pollen cones, and females produce ovules that will become the seeds. When they ripen, they're apricot colored and fleshy like fruit, but that's just the seed's soft outer coating. Female juniper cones look like fruit, too, like berries, but they're not berries, either."

We step back a moment to look at the rich, green leaves of the male above us. The neighboring tree is female, so we step that way to look for her hanging ovules.

"There's some," Susan Jane points out.

A few round shapes are visible peeking out from among the leaves. They are still green and hang mostly in pairs on the ends of long stalks.

"Soon these will fall off the tree and cover the ground beneath. I think they're really pretty lying there among the leaves. At that point, the newly formed embryos will continue to grow and develop as the seeds lie there on the ground."

"At that point they also stink," she said.

"Yes," I agree, smiling, "some people say that, especially when that fleshy outer part starts rotting away. Before that, though, they look pretty tempting to eat, like fruit!"

"Really?"

"Yes," I say, a bit embarrassed to tell my story, but I decide to continue. "Last October, my mom and I were walking here collecting leaves. The ginkgo seeds looked so pretty on the ground, so intriguing. And I didn't know much about them, so I took some home in my pocket and put them in a bowl for decoration."

"Oh no!" Susan Jane says. "Your mom has dementia and ate some, right?"

"Yes," I say ruefully, and go on to tell her the story. "I heard my mom say from the other room, 'My mouth is burning! What could be causing that?' I called back to her from the living room, 'What? Did you eat something?' My mom said, 'I don't remember! What did I eat? My mouth and throat are burning!' What, indeed!? *Ginkgo biloba* is what she ate! While she was busy at the bowl, I was just learning from my resource that ginkgos are not exactly edible. It also informed me that they are foul smelling because the flesh around the seed contains butyric acid which gives the seeds their rancid, rotten odor, like vomit. They didn't exactly strike me that way, though. The odor from the ones I picked up was definitely pungent, not terrible, but strong enough that I washed my hands after handling them—which is a good thing to do after collecting them."

"Why is that?" Susan Jane asks.

"Well, yeah, you see, it got worse as I read on, because the pulp can cause an allergic skin reaction similar to poison ivy and can be irritating to mucous membranes. Hence, why my mom now felt burning in her mouth and throat. She most certainly must have popped one of those into her mouth and eaten the soft outer part. The inner seed inside the flesh is also considered mildly toxic, apparently nutritious to eat in moderation. The seeds without the outer flesh are roasted and sold as 'ginkgo nuts.' The nuts have been used forever in Asian cuisine. Every autumn I see people gathering ginkgo seeds in the park. But you do have to roast or cook them before eating, never eat them raw, because the heat neutralizes some, not all, of the toxins."

Susan Jane nods, taking all this in. "Wow!"

"Ironically," I add, "western medicine uses an extract made from the leaves touted as helpful for improving memory and cognition!"

"Yes, it is ironic for your mom," she chuckles, "but what happened with her afterwards? Was she okay?"

"Oh, in an hour or so the burning retreated to only her mouth, and in two hours it was only her tongue, the sensation completely gone by bedtime. The next morning there were no aftereffects at all."

"Good thing!"

"Agreed!"

We continue walking across the street (as it happens toward the hackberry next), but I am thoughtful as we depart this life-affirming tree that I so love.

Early in the morning of August 6, 1945, Hiroshima's ginkgo trees were happily growing when the A-bomb dropped on the city, incinerating everything in its wake including trees. Growing less than a mile from the epicenter of the blast, one particular ginkgo tree had its trunk destroyed, but sprouted new leaves again from the roots around its base the following spring. This tree and other tree species very near ground zero that came back from near annihilation became known as survivor trees (*hibakujumoku*, in Japanese) and are honored today with memorial plaques. They are remarkable symbols of the eternal cycle of growth and renewal. They are ambassadors of enduring hope.

My dad's last breaths took place in the upstairs bedroom of the house that had been his home for 50 plus years. Two ginkgos grow on the boulevard just outside where the room overlooks. Their leaves had already turned brilliant yellow weeks earlier, and then had chosen their time to create a seemingly instant carpet of fallen leaves in a synchronized leaf drop, as is the way with ginkgos. Over the prior week, maple leaves had also fallen, as had the leaves of the little-leaf linden on the front lawn.

It was the morning of November 14th, and even we in our inexperience could see the end for my dad was near. Erling had just arrived from Aitkin, and I asked him to spend a few moments with Chet. "Go to him," I said, "he can hear you."

My sister, Julie, on her way out of the room, mentioned an apnea had just occurred, that our dad's breathing was slowing.

"Hi, Junior Weatherman," Erling was saying to my dad, along with some other quieter words I couldn't make out as I entered the room.

I walked over to the other side of the bed and spoke into my dad's left ear, the ear that worked better.

"Dad, the Senior Weatherman is here."

He nodded once, faintly. He was listening. I sensed my dad was happy to have Erling right there, his strong, sensitive presence, his camaraderie—the history for so many decades of their relationship together. My dad, my father. Chester Joseph Mirocha.

We'd been through so many clinics and visits together, and it all came down to these last moments, here, now.

My dad had once told me he was afraid a curtain of blackness would fall when he passed. This thought scared him. "No," I had immediately reassured him, "It will be light. At least, that's what people say." Perhaps because of this spoken fear, I had found myself coaching my dad over the last 24 hours, saying things like "It's okay; this is how it happens; it's a natural process."

As Erling stood up now and began to leave the room, I repeated some of these things again into my dad's ear. "You're a good man. Relax. You can let go. Enjoy the ride. It's okay. This is how it happens. It's natural. Thanks for being my dad. You are safe and warm and secure here with your family."

Erling left the room, and I went around to sit on the other side of the bed, the side my dad was facing. His eyes were half closed, but he was aware. He heard. I sensed him shift a bit as I was speaking—a shift of understanding; a letting-go feeling presented itself in the air coming from him. I sat down and took hold of his hand. All of a sudden, his head came off the pillow, his eyes opened wide, and he looked directly into mine. I was startled. Where was this energy coming from? I thought he had something to say, but of course he couldn't.

"Hi, Dad!" I said loudly, and full of joy.

He nodded a little, just slightly.

"It's Stephanie!" I wanted to make sure he knew it was me, because who knows what chemicals his body was making, what he was seeing. He nodded again, and my joy reverberated when he heard and recognized me. His blue eyes were big and beautiful, and they blazed with brilliance, never straying from mine. I quietly sat there smiling, gazing back.

After a few seconds, his eyes began to appear without emotion, not neutral either, but just wide, light filled and infinite like the sky. That's what I thought of later. Looking at the sky on my walk later was exactly the way his eyes looked then. They appeared innocent, trusting, gazing as if transfixed until I began to feel my own become a conduit to someplace else. I held his look all through this wondrous releasing of light from within and out of his eyes exactly like the luminous sky, vast, wide, and wholly filled and into which that light released. Then, his head fell heavily back onto the pillow, eyes half closed again now glassy, lifeless, and dull looking.

All of this happened so fast that I could still hear Erling's footsteps going down the wooden stairs. I got up and went around to his "good ear" again and listened to his breath, observing how it was becoming very shallow, and light and ethereal to nonexistent. Another apnea occurred. My body tensed. Wait a minute! It was all happening so fast; I felt it now. I felt him leaving.

Everyone should be up here!

In that split second, I decided to give other people the opportunity to be here, a thought Dad would have agreed with, even though I had to leave his side to get them. I ran to the railing just as Erling reached the bottom stair.

"Get people up here, now," I yelled frantically, then ran back, listening, thinking, "Is this it?"

Of course, it was. It was just hard for me to understand. I had never watched someone die before. I hovered over him, noting the stillness to his body as the breathing became a gentle wisp of air, barely noticeable, a flutter of a dragonfly wing, a grass stem in the breeze by the cabin lake shore, a nothing.

Julie arrived upstairs first. I was glad. She noticed a gulp, or last gasp, and then with his family all around him, his last breath of air flew away outward into that waiting light, into the universe. I kept listening, saying, "Is he still breathing?" It was hard for me to accept.

"No, he's gone," Julie said.

We watched him, felt his skin, held his hands, knew he was gone. Only a shell was left, a tent to be folded up and put away. He had left the body he didn't need anymore. That's what he would have said. "I don't need this anymore. It doesn't matter now."

I have found a thing that endures: the wind pushing air into every crevice of a rock face, the same thing as my breath pulling oxygen into every capillary of my body, and into the heart. And therein lies another abiding thing. Love.

Fanned to life with breath and air. Awake, aware, love needs no improvement, no upgrade, no change. It is its own creative life force, sufficient and enough. On immutable wings it floats, simple and free, upon streams of sunlight into everything.

The body is a temporary thing. That is a given. Eventually, it gets left behind, is no longer needed to enjoy the view. When that time comes, we need only use it for one last hike up, climbing the mountain as high as possible before stepping into air the color of azure blue. In my imagination, I make this ascent as far as I can go until I meet the place where rock meets sky. Beyond that, I cannot step, at least not yet, not before my own time comes. Instead, I sit in quiet contemplation, perched up there on my mountain top, my mind's eye watching sunlight sinking into dusk. My gaze descends to the valley below where pinpricks of light from the houses blink back up at me and into the night sky, far away to the horizon. The twinkling scene lifts across the hills like sparkling glints of a million eyes reflecting back the universe of stars above in the glance of a million others.

"Godspeed!" I whisper into that soothing darkness, inadvertently getting Susan Jane's attention as we finish crossing the street.

Chapter 11
Hackberry
(Genus *Celtis*)
GALAXIES CROSSING

North America is home to several species of native hackberry trees which, taken together, appear all across North America from southern parts of Canada, in every state, and into Mexico. The fruit is sweet and nutritious, varying in color when ripe from orange to deep purple depending on the species. Common hackberry (Celtis occidentalis) *has the largest range, preferring areas of deciduous forests, riverbanks, and floodplains everywhere except the far western states, Louisiana, and Florida. Other species of hackberry easily fill in those niches. Sugarberry* (Celtis laevigata) *is located mainly in the south while its neighbor, dwarf hackberry, continues north into Canada. Desert hackberry thrives in the dry, rocky soils and gravelly washes of the Sonoran landscape and other similar soil types such as in central Florida, offering hackberry's typically delectable stone fruit for wildlife to feast on. Netleaf hackberry takes over from desert hackberry moving west and northward up the Pacific coast.*

EACH TREE IS A WORLD UNTO ITSELF. IN THE BIG PICTURE, EACH TREE IS A galaxy of life gravitating around other galaxies, looping through the universe. We are all made of the same stuff, just that some stuff tastes better than others and feeds different species. What is toxic or disgustingly foul to one, can be healthy, nutritious, and even delicious to another. The scientific database reveals general patterns from which to extrapolate. Evidence can verify postulations and theories, but no "galaxy" provides an uncomplicated, black-and-white rule to describe it all. In the midst of this (or perhaps because of this), everything has its own, unique beauty, from the smallest speck to the highest mountain—wind, weather, rock, wing, human, slug, fungi, and so on, to infinity. All is imbibed with love pouring from the sky above and coming from the earth below, enduring while warmly reassuring the connectedness of each one to the other.

Trees offer a fascinating, endless exploration of other living beings. How much water they drink at night vs. during the day. How sweet their sap is, and what factors vary that sap's sugar content today as opposed to yesterday. How biological responses change depending on the weather, the time of day or night, the stressors faced, the interactions with helpful fungi as well as with fungi that harm. What hormones are released seasonally. What the timing is for leaf drop in fall and bud burst in spring.

Trees provide food sources for a multitude of creatures, not only mammals and birds (which may come to mind first), but also for amphibians and insects. One warm spring day, I spotted a cecropia moth as I was exiting the grocery store. Newly emerged from its cocoon, this exquisitely lovely moth lay on the cement not far from the brusquely grating wheels of my grocery cart rolling by. Knowing he would not be able to move until his wings dried, I gently encouraged him (it was a male) to walk onto my finger and then took him with me, placing the moth on the dashboard of my car. In this way, we both completed our business—I ran errands, and he finished drying.

When he was ready, my daughter and I watched the cecropia flutter up past the porch and waft away over the roof. Unlike most adult butterflies and moths, he will eat nothing; he cannot physically do so. His only quest was to use his over-sized, sensitive antennae to pick up the pheromones of a female cecropia ladylove waiting within a mile or so, meet up with her, and mate. Good luck, my friend!

Caterpillars rely on specific host plants to nourish themselves and grow. One of my favorite butterflies, the mourning cloak, loves the leaves of elm, willow, poplar, and hackberry. Somehow, the female butterfly knows just what plant is right to lay her eggs on, enabling her offspring to emerge and start chomping away. Some butterflies and moths are so specialized with a tree species as sole host that they are named after the tree, such as the hackberry emperor butterfly (*Asterocampa celtis*). Besides its emperor, hackberry serves up a leaf buffet to two more specialists, the tawny emperor and American snout butterflies. Others, such as the cecropia moth, thrive on dozens of different plants as hosts and do just fine. While, for example, an oak tree hosts over 500 species of moths, butterflies, and other insects, nonnative species like ginkgo host less than ten. This is another reason why native plants are so important to conserve. Plants do not exist alone. They exist, like all of us, within the web of life. Many forms of life rely upon the insects who rely upon those specific plants for feeding themselves and their offspring.

When I stand next to a tree and observe, for instance, an ant going about its business traveling up and down the contours of one deeply furrowed ridge of bark, a feeling of calm happiness descends on me. Here is an ant on the tree where it belongs.

Everything is as it should be.

Let's enter the world of the hackberry, a.k.a. common hackberry (*Celtis occidentalis*), in the Hemp family. Notice how the alternatively growing branches are covered with deep green, simple (not compound) leaves. The edges, or margins, of the ovate leaves are serrated, and the leaf comes to a sharply-pointed tip. For a moment, let's find a spot on this September day beneath the tree to take a break and rest for a while. The hackberry tree's presence reveals itself as wonderfully quiet and restful. A safe place. Dangling from every branch amidst the fluttering leaves are reddish-purple, round little fruits about the size of a small pea. A bird over there has one of them in his beak right now! A robin! And there's a cedar waxwing, perhaps just come from the juniper grove with the taste of a different sort of blue tidbit lingering on the palate. A squirrel far above us is snacking as well, nibbling whatever he can reach. He could store some, and perhaps does, but his experience has taught him there is no need. Hackberry fruits have a high sugar content in their skin as well as a tendency toward dryness which preserves them and allows them to linger on the tree all through winter, remaining perfectly edible. Perhaps sometime in the cold weather ahead, a deer will come through and browse to the level where her head can reach. Whether an animal is revving up for winter, or about to migrate, or finding preserved food ready for plucking over the next few months, this is the right place to be.

Hackberry fruits are actually not berries. In botany, they are called drupes. A drupe's innermost ovary layer (the endocarp) surrounds and protects the single seed kernel, forming a strong, stony pit around it. In a berry, this layer would be very thin and flexible, and there would be more than one seed inside. Other examples of drupes are plums, peaches, apricots, olives, cherries, and almonds. Hackberry fruits are edible, but don't chew them; the seed inside is too hard. I like to pick one or two for fun while I'm walking and suck on the sweet, pulpy outer part, then spit out the rest when I'm done. It's really delicious. The great thing about hackberries is that the whole thing is edible and nutritious, even the hard, inner seed if you grind it up.

Pluck a hackberry and enjoy the flavor of one of the oldest known plant foods humans have eaten for thousands of years. Hackberry drupes are fantastically nutritious, packed with calories derived from proteins, carbohydrates, and fats. They also contain vitamins and minerals including calcium carbonate and magnesium. Crush with a mortar and pestle, add to water, let sit overnight, then strain to make a drink. The Dakota people traditionally dry and pound them into a condiment used for seasoning meat. The Chahiksichahiks (Pawnee) mix pounded hackberries with a little fat and parched corn, which sounds good to me as a useful snack item at home as well as for traveling. The list of Indigenous Peoples preparing hackberries is long.

Archeological digs often turn up the very hard, stony seed pits of hackberries, for these tend to hang around. Similar to the rough surface of a peach pit, the hackberry seed is coated with a protective latticework. The microscopic holes of this structure are stuffed with calcium carbonate. The amazing thing is, the latticework itself is composed of the same chemical composition as the gemstone opal, albeit in minute quantities. On learning of Dr. Hope Jahren's research that led to this remarkable discovery, my image of the hackberry has changed considerably. My imagination now visualizes a profusion of drupes penetrating from every level of the hackberry tree as a constellation of stars shining their opalescence out into the night along with the moon and starlight.

Standing within our hackberry tree world, you might notice little nubs growing on the underside of many leaves. These green, protruding growths are called hackberry nipple galls and are formed from an insect that relies on the hackberry tree for its entire life cycle. Called hackberry psyllids (pronounced "SILL-ids," *Pachypsylla* genus) these insects mate and lay eggs in spring. The eggs hatch and nymphs emerge to suck the sap from the leaves. Galls form from host tissue growing around and enclosing the insect inside. In late summer and fall, adults emerge from the gall to seek shelter in bark and leaf litter where they overwinter before completing their life cycle in the next spring's mating season. The psyllids get a place to live unless a squirrel eats the gall as a healthy snack first! Many other creatures join in the buffet, especially during the exposed stages of the insects during spring and fall. Ants, flies, and spiders eat the psyllid eggs in springtime and also in autumn during the adult emergence stage. All this insect activity also attracts songbirds which is especially helpful as it coincides with their seasonal migrations. Juvenile bluebirds in the fall gearing up for their first flight are just one of the many species of songbirds enjoying the nutritional benefits of hackberry fruits along with the proteins derived from consuming insects—all from the same tree. Hungry gray tree frogs, toads, and lizards also sit down to dine in this busy café. The insect enticements are not lost on the hackberry's evolutionary tactics to ensure dispersal of its seeds, a strategy that mutually benefits everyone. The world within a hackberry galaxy is truly filled with a plethora of life.

Hackberries, however, are not the only hosts for insect gall inducers. Galls are common on many plants, and, in fact, insects are not the only causes. Mites, fungi, dwarf mistletoe, and bacteria weigh in here, and each species prefers its own, particular host. Oaks support more than 200 gall-producing insects alone. The linden gall mite, the goldenrod gall fly, the jumping oak gall, the Cooley spruce gall and cedar apple rust (fungi induced) are just a few colorful names for these invaders that arrive clad in their own unique regalia ready to create some oftentimes wildly interesting, abstract shapes. In general, galls do not usually affect the overall health of the plants they invade, although they don't exactly help either. The wonderful result of galls, however, and their associated insects reveals itself in the seasonal food provisions they supply for other species, adding to each plant's particular, vibrant offering within the web of life.

One of the notes of condolence I received after my dad died was an email from a former Environment Committee member who had served with my dad. Attached to the email was a photo. The photo she sent was so unexpected and yet so comforting to receive during that difficult time that it filled me with gratitude. Her short note accompanied a photo of what my dad had told her was his favorite tree in the park. I didn't know he had a favorite tree in the park! Or if I did, it was only vague background information that I didn't log on enough to find out which tree. The photo was recent. Snow lies all around the darkly contrasting trunk in the photo, but the highly recognizable bark of the hackberry stands out. Warty, textured, corky, deeply ridged, and curving this way and that like contour lines on a topo map—these are all ways to describe the hackberry tree's signature bark. The tree in the photo is, naturally, one of his tagged trees.

If I had any remaining doubts about the origins of those red metal tags of a different era that I was sporadically discovering on my forays through the park, they were put to rest the day my brother, Andrew, told me one of the trees in my parents' backyard was a tagged hackberry. He told me this, actually, the day of my first Tree Trek, right after I returned to the house and showed off my mulberry-stained hands to both my mom and him.

"We've got those," Andrew said looking at my berry-stained hands, "They're hackberries. Mom and I have been picking them all morning. She really likes fruit!"

"What? We have a hackberry tree?"

"Yes, it even has a label Dad nailed onto it."

"But those can't be hackberries. It's June! They're not even ripe yet," I said. "Wait, I'll be right back."

Immediately, I went outside to investigate this mystery. As it turns out, both a mulberry *and* a hackberry grow back there. On the hackberry, nailed up for all to see was another red metal ID tag. Following the line of the hackberry trunk upwards, I saw how its branches could easily be confused with connecting to the mulberry branches, now dripping with thousands of berries (not true berries, incidentally!). Both trees are actually growing in the neighbor's yard, not ours. The branches laden with juicy mulberries hang into our yard over a short fence, making it easy to pick their low hanging fruit. On the other tree, the hackberry, I saw where my dad had reached over the fence to nail on the tag; it was a surreal, slightly shocking feeling to discover this large, healthy tree had been growing there most of my life completely unknown to me while it matter-of-factly continued going about its business of being a hackberry tree, calmly orbiting within its own galaxy of life. Now, finally, the two of us had intersected.

After explaining to my brother and my mom that he'd simply mistaken the mulberry branch as ending up on the hackberry tree, the three of us went back out with containers to pick more mulberries. Mulberry trees in production are truly extravagant—even profligate in the way their unpicked fruit goes to waste. Overripe berries littered the ground beneath our feet and dyed the grass a purplish black. We stepped all over them and stained our shoes in the process, but the reward was worth the effort!

My dad's favorite tree in the park grows very near the lake. I have no idea why it was his favorite. He never shared that with me. In fact, his committee colleagues don't know either. I could speculate that when the new, 4x6 hackberry tags came in, my dad pulled the old red one off his favorite tree in the park and transferred it to the tree in the backyard. It's a rational explanation, but I don't know if that's correct. It doesn't matter. A few mysteries are healthy to keep around, and there is something to be said about the importance of realizing when you should simply stop looking.

Worlds collide and intersect whether made up of the tiniest atoms or the largest galaxies. They morph and change one another as they collide, often to the point of no return. Parts glom on, others explode things into detritus, and still others manage to stay neutral moving through the whole chaos. People do the same thing, just living their lives. When thought, image, and emotion collide inside a person, such unexpected moments can snap the mind into the present, waking one into an instant of being fully alive that can forever leave an imprint.

This happened to me toward the end of one of my fall Tree Treks. I had just completed my remarks at our last stop, the black walnut (*Juglans nigra*), where we were grouped together on the pedestrian bridge. This bridge, by the way, provides a much-needed access point connecting the lake area to the rest of the park. No longer do pedestrians and bicyclists have to worry about crossing through the busy traffic below. Another benefit is the branches of the black walnut grow right next to the railing on the north side, in effect bringing us into the heart of the tree where all the action is taking place.

Consequently, I usually stop here to point out to the group the distinctive leaf scars of the black walnut. They are super easy to identify, and a great place to start for those who want to learn winter tree ID. A black walnut's leaf scar presents a very charming face with a sort of widow's peak and a big smile that, once learned, is easily recognizable. We usually don't stay long, though. Traffic noise is one reason, but also the fact that many people use this bridge and there isn't a lot of room for our group of 20 or more to spread out.

We were just approaching the bridge's apex when someone in the group called out, "Make room. Wheels coming!"

A very fit, athletic man was just entering on the end behind us where the tagged black locust grows, heading our way. He was tooling along on cross country roller skis and taking up a good amount of space with his poling action. Relaxed and in control, he was also clearly an accomplished skier. I immediately thought of my dad who used to do this same activity during the summer and autumn months training for winter trips ahead. Some of those trips, such as out in Colorado, involved serious backcountry mountain skiing and, if one is going to race (which my dad also did), the sport requires endurance training in the non-snow months. When my dad was done with his roller skis, he gave them to me. I used them one summer, rolling about town rather conspicuously, I should add. I may be the first and only person in our very small, rural town ever to roller ski along the bike paths getting ready for the winter season.

All these thoughts and memories flashed through my mind as I watched the roller skier approach. I paused and smiled as we made way for him.

What he said next, without a doubt, made apparent what observations were forming in his own mind as he approached our group. I considered his point of view. He was seeing a woman with binoculars around her neck (incidentally, the same ones my dad used) and gesturing toward a tree branch, leaning over the railing with people gathered around her. This may be why, as he moved through the center of our group, he called out wholeheartedly,

"If this is Chet Mirocha's Tree Trek continuing on, great work! Keep it going!"

My mouth gaped open in surprise. He knew Chet was no longer with us. He knew this was Tree Trek! More than that, his genuine air of positivity instantly transferred into me a feeling of everything coalescing into one of those indelible moments. Joy flowed through me. This was the right place to be, indeed, and I was doing exactly what I needed to be doing.

Everything was as it should be.

All I could think to call to his receding back was, "I'm Stephanie Mirocha!"

He did not reply. He simply kept rolling on. Our gap closed, and we continued crossing. In quiet astonishment, I watched our roller skier round the apex of the bridge until he flowed down the other side and vanished. I don't know how or if he even knew my dad. Maybe he skied with him. It doesn't matter. What matters is the wake that formed from our two paths crossing spread out through me in waves of exhilaration.

On the other side of the bridge, I turned to the group and made some concluding remarks. We were out of time. "Thank you so much, everyone, for joining me today!"

I bowed in grateful respect as they thanked me in return.

Everything is as it should be.

Chapter 12

Seed-bearing Plants

(Spermatophytes)

Listening

Some of the most essential life forms on our planet, seed-bearing plants shape the soil and provide boundless resources including vast supplies of food. Spermatophytes are divided into two major groups, nonflowering and flowering, both of which reproduce by means of male pollen and female ovules. Nonflowering trees, the gymnosperm group with their naked ovules, emerged about 300 million years ago from the ancient (now extinct) seed ferns. Gymnosperms bear seed cones and often appear as evergreens. The other group, the flowering plants (angiosperms) with their protected ovules within a flower's ovary, date back to the Early Cretaceous over 100 million years ago, each species evolving its own flower pollination strategy. Overall, angiosperms bear a spectacular variety of fruit and are the dominant seed-bearing plants on earth.

MASTER NATURALIST TRAINING WEEK BEGAN LIKE ANY WEEK-LONG TRAINING: with an ice breaker. We were a varied group of 25 people from all walks of life. Educators, retirees, camp counselors, a couple artists (including myself), two interns, and a former wildfire fighter, ranging in age from 20 to 70, and all joined in a common purpose through our love of and respect for nature. We are part of a great tribe, and we needed to get to know each other.

On the floor in the front of the room, our session leader spread a blanket out and began to lay a variety of artifacts on it. She tossed feathers, an arrowhead, a nest, pinecones, stones, a basket, animal hides, antlers—about 12 nature-related things. Next, she instructed us to come up as a group and choose one item without thinking about it too much, to just grab whatever resonated with us on a first impression. She explained there were two of everything, and after we made our choice, we should find and team up with the other person who had chosen our twin object. After telling our new partner what drew us to our matching objects and exchanging our stories, we would then come back as a group and each team would tell the other's story to the group.

It was a wonderful concept, and all would have gone perfectly well, except things worked out a bit differently for me.

We approached en masse to look over the artifacts. A huge pinecone immediately caught my eye. It was about 18 inches long, massive compared with pinecones native to our region in the Midwest. I knew this was a cone from a sugar pine (*Pinus lambertiana*) from out west, and that it was well within the usual size range for the huge cones these pines produce. The front porch of my childhood home held a sugar pine cone on the brick sill all my years growing up. In fact, it's still there. I knew it was from a sugar pine, because as a child I had learned this from my dad. I looked around for who else was holding a sugar pine cone until my eyes landed on a pleasant-looking woman with silver hair and a kind smile standing on the far side of the now empty blanket. Like me, she was holding her pinecone in two hands.

"Is this a sugar pine cone?" I asked the instructor on my way over to join my new acquaintance.

"I don't know," she replied. "It could be."

"Oh, well, actually I know that it is!" I replied, happily holding the object I had so warmly gravitated toward, not yet having learned the concept that as naturalists we are guides, not expected to be experts.

I met my partner Linda and began to tell my story first. I would have told her about the sugar pine cone living on the front porch sill, how long it had been part of my childhood landscape. The meaning it had for me, especially reminding me of my dad because he loved trees. How it brought to mind many shared hikes with him in the forest or swishing along cross country ski trails in the winter. He had picked it up in a phase of life before I was born, most likely on an outing with his young family while living in Davis, California where he earned his PhD. It had managed to survive three moves the family made after that, to North Carolina where I was born and then two more in Minnesota to its current home for the last 60 years.

I was just getting to the part about how it reminded me of my dad and our hikes, when Linda interrupted me. "Are you related to Chet Mirocha?" she asked, looking at my name tag.

"Well, yes, he's my dad," I replied. "He passed away a couple months ago. Did you know him?"

"Yes, I did, and I'm so sorry," she said. "I read it in the ski newsletter."

Ski newsletter! That pricked my attention. Something in me stirred and shifted. It turned out she knew him very well, had been with him on group ski trips climbing up the mountains to huts in Colorado. She described how the slope was so steep with such icy conditions they had to use special ski skins on the base of their skis for grip. It was an extreme, adventure type of skiing involving Telemark ski turns down the mountainside through powder snow. My dad was an expert at Telemarking and enjoyed sharing his technique with the group. Always a teacher! Linda explained that this type of adventure was very hard on her knees, and she eventually had to stop going. She knew him, in other words, very well. An experience like that shared among ten people or so for days on end in a small hut up in the mountains creates bonds for a lifetime. It turns out she was one of a core group of people who accompanied my dad on many ski trips in Minnesota as well, including to our family cabin. I had never heard her name even mentioned! This was all a complete surprise.

She went on to explain that my dad, especially on the Rocky Mountain hut-to-hut trips, was a ski mentor to her. Linda wasn't just a casual acquaintance of his, and upon realizing this fact, I basically lost my composure. It was suddenly all too much to take in. The loss of my dad was just too recent. I wasn't ready for this. A wave of overwhelming grief swept through me at that moment and did not let go. Seeing this, she drew me into her arms for a hug, and as I rested against her shoulder, I blurted out, "I just can't bear it. I miss him so much. I don't know what to do!"

The next moment I was weeping uncontrollably on her shoulder. She held me briefly, and then we stood apart as I attempted to do what we were asked, choking the rest of my pinecone story out. All the other teams were chattering, casually enjoying the session, getting to know each other. What a contrast to the deep intensity I felt and the altered state I had now entered! The awkwardness of the situation was quite apparent, along with Linda's helplessness at being able to console me. She was here to train, just like me, and we didn't even know each other! What was she supposed to do? I attempted to collect myself, and she listened compassionately to the rest of my pinecone story. Then she took her turn.

Linda's story was so similar to mine it actually made me feel better, made me laugh even at how this object united us. It was truly amazing how that pinecone brought us together! Everyone remarked on it later after we shared this with the group, how extraordinary it was for two people unknown to each other who, coincidentally, shared such a strong association with my father, to meet in this way! Linda finished by saying the sugar pine cone brought back memories of her dad as well, of times shared on their hikes where he lived out west, how he taught her what he knew about trees and nature every time she visited.

Our fathers, we agreed, nurtured our love of the outdoors.

"Did you know this was a sugar pine cone?" I asked.

"No," she said, "but I'm glad I do now!"

The rest of the training week for me was lonely and emotionally exhausting after such a traumatic start. I recovered somewhat, of course. Projects, outings, and nature-based learning filled me with enthusiasm. Still, try as I may to thrust it aside, a background feeling of being lost, vulnerable, unsure of myself, and cut off from everyone persisted. Each night I returned to my dorm room, which isn't the same as going home.

I learned something from going through the experience, for it underscored the importance of the caring connections that exist within ourselves and to each other. Finding our purpose in life, our meaningful way to express the wisdom, gifts, and passion we each have coming from within to share, these things rise above the chatter and distractions of daily life. These things, it seems, are all that really matter in the end.

Nature welcomes us every day, waiting to bestow sustenance and calm on those who take contemplative action by immersing themselves in her open arms. Listening to peoples' stories has taught me about the many and varied ways to arrive at these timeless places of resilience. Mostly this involves people following their passions for activities that usually take place outdoors. Snowmobiling for hours on end can be calming and meaningful. The same can be said for running a marathon, climbing a mountain, taking a walk, or getting your gear out for fishing, rafting, canoeing, or biking. Each of these outdoor experiences comes with a culture, fresh air, and obstacles to negotiate, methods and techniques to learn. They teach us about our strengths, and through them we find purpose as well as relaxation.

One art customer of mine told a story that remains prominent in my mind. Deer hunting one autumn, this man was alone, sitting quietly with his rifle propped on the shooting rest, waiting high up in a deer stand. A soft snowfall had begun, and the cold started creeping into his bones, but still he sat because that's all part of hunting. In the almost effervescent quietude, he began to notice the surrounding forest sounds reverberating, including the tiny patter sound of each individual snowflake's landing. All at once, a chickadee plunked down on the end of his gun barrel and started to sing. My painting of the chickadee in the snowfall reminded him of the moment that had suddenly filled him with such surprised joy at simply being alive in the world!

Erling tells the story of fishing in Alaska one day on the Chilkoot River. After about half an hour, he turned at a small noise coming from behind him, only to find several brown bears all this time had been feasting on berries not far away, calmly minding their own business. Not interested in him at all! A friend reminisces about the rare talks with his father that arose from sitting in a bird blind for hours together, happening once a year. I can see the result of the many one-on-one talks my daughter shared with her dad during the two-hour drives to baseball games down and back from the Cities. I hold close to my heart the oft-repeated banter between my dad and me, skiing and discussing who goes first down the next hill. I hear the deeper story in my husband's reminiscence of fishing for perch in the bay, just he and his dad—the two of them—unaware of any medical diagnosis, both of them finding out later those hours of precious time are what they had and what they would hold onto. All these experiences cannot be undone. All of these experiences inform us.

The day after my dad died, I walked in the park toward the lake, needing some alone time in a place I love. I didn't get far before I collapsed with grief on the walking path, swept under a tsunami of personal loss. A passerby compassionately offered me her dog to pet because she recognized what I was suffering, because she had been through this same thing herself, she said. Her dog offered himself to me in a furry sideways stance, and as I gratefully petted him, I heard the "hank-hank" call of a nearby songbird, a nuthatch. In that instant, I became aware of the beauty of the day's setting sun filling the sky to the west across the water. These things were stark reminders of the fact that everything was going on business as usual, neutrally, and that was okay!

The world's artifacts speak to us from their lowly position tossed onto a blanket. But speak to us they do, loudly and clearly, of our emotions and our life experiences. They are the stuff from which we are formed. They are what binds us to each other and to ourselves. These sensory objects we can pick up, feel, taste, smell, and listen to are essential to our existence. They are us, for we arise from nature. Without them we are nothing.

"Spermatophyte" is a scientific term referring to the largest group of all existing plants, including trees (and other seed-bearing plants), and the place they occupy in nature. Almost 300 years ago, the scientist, Carl Linnaeus, created the taxonomic system of classification so that we could talk with a common understanding about life on earth, in all its evolving diversity from the past into present, in our search for knowledge of the world around us. Taxonomy, however, is an abstract tool that does not give us any experience at all of what it's like to live within the present moment using all our senses to become aware of our surroundings in the actual world. It requires us to live in our heads a little while as a starting point before setting out into the field in the sunshine.

Virtual reality, social media feeds, internet content, and the evolving world of artificial intelligence (AI) taken as a group provide an analogy to Linnaeus's abstract tool with one essential addition. These digital tools require us to temporarily give up our birthright of autonomy unlike what we naturally receive in the come-what-may events happening in the actual world of nature.

Understood and accepted as entertainment only or as carefully vetted learning tools, these can even become additional treasured objects of our experience. Yet, that key distinction exists, easy to miss within that analogy, and it is a crucial one. It turns on the fact that Linnaeus is as neutral as a bird song heard by chance on a spring morning compared with the unknown person or software whose job it is to manipulate and track, for example, content usage, or to decide what to feed and portray in their programming. What comes up is not just random, because the latter almost always involves some sort of intent, such as power advantage or monetary gain by funneling the user into an experience that precludes their own spontaneity and clouds their intuition. An individual granting any deeper meaning to the content they receive as actually shaping and defining their identity disengages them from the track leading naturally to true self-discovery—and even to truth itself—and may even derail into a place cut off from reality, languishing in isolation. AI at higher levels asks us to relinquish our autonomy to an evolving thing that is utterly cut off from nature and therefore from the love infusing and uniting nature with us. In addition, AI darkly threatens to deaden the intellect altogether by closing doors to our own intuition and ability to build creative brain connections—an ability that takes work and practice.

Life feeds us random connections and interesting bits that resonate within our inner selves, and in those introspective moments we may find ourselves searching for ways to put those pieces together. The bigger picture is always there, offering that opportunity, waiting for us to pay attention. Being outdoors in nature is an essential part of this. Our actual world is where we find our real sense of presence in and among ourselves.

In the midst of this, of course, we need trees! Without trees, we wouldn't survive. This not only applies in a biological sense (oxygen, for starters) but also on an emotional level. For trees can inspire us to share our vital, personal stories.

Trees are out there awaiting discovery in everyday places, from the most obscure trail to paved, public walkways. Along the way, someday a certain tree may resonate with you. Learn more about your tree. Visit when you can. Listen to what it has to say. In doing so, you will most likely learn something about yourself as well. You might even hear from that deepest self that has been waiting for you to take notice. Trees have much to teach us on many levels. Trees have helped me tell my story, and they are great storytellers in their own right. They can translate the most mundane scenario into mighty sagas and epics in ways we are helpless at times to understand directly without them. Through my grief, trees have been my expert guides and support. The experience has bound us even closer into lifelong friendships I rely upon. I certainly cannot take for granted such magnanimous life partners!

Hard science provides naturalists (whether seasoned or just starting out) the unshakeable framework for our work as educators, advocates, data collectors and compilers, researchers, citizen scientists, and lifelong learners. The more we get into it, the more passionate we may become. In fact, when we sit down at the table together, coming from our diverse perspectives and begin to converse, that's when things really start to get interesting!

I grew up with a tree-loving father. He naturally infused this into the culture of the family household, such as the day he rolled a 20-inch-diameter ponderosa pine tree stump up the front steps, through the porch, and into its rightful place dominating the fireplace hearth. A fixture of my childhood, it was (and still remains) just like any other well-used piece of furniture. Ever since I can remember that stump has offered a welcoming surface to set objects on, to set up the annual Christmastime crèche, to take photos of the new kittens looking over the edges, or to just sit on to warm up by the fire.

The Norway maple of my girlhood was my first tree friend. Climbing its strong, sinewy branches, I often stopped to inhale their scent on my way to the upper canopy. A dry, almost invisible coating of maple tree slough, not exactly dirt, lingered on my hands. I liked this feeling and expected it. On windy days, I made a point of climbing as high as I could to take my "seat," a crook in the forking branches up top. As the wind swayed limbs and girl, I would close my eyes and feel part of the tree, reveling in the safety and warmth I felt within those particular branches. Visiting my childhood home years later as an adult and mother, my maple tree often got a hug.

For years, a particular eastern white pine in the current town where I live has poured down grace and energy flowing into me whenever I walk beneath it. I feel this as a physical, tingling sensation. Oftentimes, I wrap my arms around its trunk as far as I can reach. Sometimes I engage in what I refer to as "tree breathing," a meditative, circular energy practice of unity with the tree. In spring, I can almost taste the spiciness of the hormones this white pine emanates. For these, and many other lifetime encounters with trees, I am grateful. They generously bestow their loving presence without fail on the creatures clambering up them and lingering beneath them. They do this equally for those who cherish them as well as for those who would destroy them. They have no choice, after all, for they cannot exactly run away!

Learning the science and dendrology of each tree species has expanded that connectedness. Strange to say, not long ago I used to take winter tree buds completely for granted. I didn't think about them much at all except as those pointy things on winter twigs all looking the same. Now, their shape, arrangement, and color have blossomed into a new perspective, offering clues to the enjoyable challenge of winter tree identification. Walking in a forest, a renewed sense of joyful recognition fills me at each tree that garners my attention for whatever reason that particular day, as if greeting a friend. This deeper understanding has enriched me and strengthened that friendship.

I have come full circle on my walk through grief. Like seasons, that grief circle doesn't ever end, it just continues into another year's season. However, the perspective I now bring to that circle has changed and widened. This is why, as I start another round, I walk with newfound hope, peace, and renewal. Although my dad will always be with me no matter where I am, nature has made a space for me to find meaning in an actual place where I can cherish his memory, walk with him through those particular trees, and keep him close to my heart. I found that place in a city park nearby to where I grew up and that will never change. But what I have also found on this round that will continue into the next goes far beyond this. It starts within myself, grounded and strong, and from there I carry that sense of place to every other feature, terrain, and topography that for some reason, someday, might call me over with a story to tell, or something new to teach. And this can be anywhere on earth.

Crossing the grass on my way home, perhaps, walking beneath a tree on a windy winter day, I might hear marcescent leaves rattling on the branches above me. These are the types of leaves that wither but remain attached and persist on the tree well into winter. I might look up. What leaves are these? Are they opposite or alternate? It's automatic now. On the ground, the familiar shape of a maple leaf might present itself, returning my gaze. Sugar maples exhibit marcescence, I now know. That bark, dark in color, deeply textured, mature, so beautiful. The voice of my own words of wisdom speak to me from deep within, empowered, as if it were the voice of the tree itself exclaiming, "Where have you been all this time? So glad to see you!"

"Sugar Maple!" I announce in glad recognition.

Warmth, safety and happiness suffuse me. In getting to know trees, I have also found myself.

I am home.

Acknowledgments

Heartfelt thanks to my husband, Erling Ellison, for his continuous support beginning the moment I disappeared into the forest of words not knowing what would emerge, reading more than one draft, and offering comments helpful in crafting a readable structure. I'm deeply grateful to Jim Perlman, publisher of Holy Cow! Press, for his belief in my work and for his bringing this book to light. His ideas and caring focus on details smoothed the way ahead at every turn. Thanks and appreciation to Felicia Schneiderhan for her editing skills and insights leading toward the best end result. I warmly thank David Unowsky, Springboard for the Arts, for his enthusiastic encouragement, which helped move what at first seemed like mountains. My daughter, Sonia Ellison, is always there for me shining a light on the trail, and I am grateful. Many thanks to Shevek McKee, Michael Kuchta and the District 10 Environment Committee who made boots-on-the-ground Tree Treks possible. Last but not least, I thank Susan Jane Cheney for her support and friendship.

Author's Note

Readers wishing to find out more about the trees on Como Park Tree Trek's self-guided trail can find my detailed write-ups for each species, *Meet the Trees,* on District 10's website: *https://district10comopark.org/tree-trek/#top*. The map is also located here.

Bibliography

IUCN. 2024. The IUCN Red List of Threatened Species. Version 2024-1. https://www.iucnredlist.org.

"BONAP'S North American Plant Atlas." Edited by John T. Kartesz, *2014 Bonap North American Plant Atlas*, 2014, bonap.net/napa.

"Keystone Plants by Ecoregion." *National Wildlife Federation*, 2024, www.nwf.org/Garden-for-Wildlife/About/Native-Plants/keystone-plants-by-ecoregion.

"Landscape Plants." Edited by Patrick Breen, *What Should It Be Called? The Paths to the Common and Botanical Names of Douglas-Fir,* Oregon State University, College of Agricultural Sciences, 2024.

"Minnesota Wildflowers." Edited by Katy Chayka, *Minnesota Wildflowers: A Field Guide to the Flora of Minnesota*, 2024, www.minnesotawildflowers.info/.

Alfs, Matthew. *Edible & Medicinal Wild Plants of the Midwest*. Minnesota Historical Society Press, 2020.

Armstrong, Wayne P. "To Be or Not To Be a Gall." *Wayne's Word; Plant Galls*, 2002, www.waynesword.net/pljuly99.htm.

Barnett, Guertin P. and Denny E.G. Schaffer. "USA National Phenology Network Botany Primer." *USA-NPN Education and Engagement Series*, 2015, www.usanpn.org/.

Borge, Mary Anne. "Hackberry, Butterflies and Birds." *The Natural Web*, 2 Mar. 2019.

Broberg, Gunnar. "The Guardian Tree: The Birthplace of Carl Linnaeus." *Princeton University Press*, The Trustees of Princeton University, 23 July 2023.

Brown, Peter M. "Rocky Mountain Tree-Ring Research." *RMTRR OLDLIST*, 2024, www.rmtrr.org/oldlist.htm.

Crane, Peter R. *Ginkgo: The Tree That Time Forgot*. Yale University Press, 2013.

Enescu, Cristian Mihai, Daniele de Rigo, et al. "Pinus Nigra in Europe: Distribution, Habitat, Usage and Threats." *European Atlas of Forest Tree Species*, 2016.

Gilmore, Melvin R., and Hugh C. Cutler. *Uses of Plants by the Indians of the Missouri River Region*. University of Nebraska Press, 1977.

Hahn, Jeffrey, and Mark Ascerno. "Insect and Mite Galls." *UMN Extension*, 2024, extension.umn.edu/yard-and-garden-insects/insect-and-mite-galls.

Hines, Chance H. "The Effects of Hackberry Psyllids on Refueling Migratory Songbirds and Autumnal Seed Rain." *ODU Digital Commons*, 2020.

Jahren, A. Hope, et al. "Biomineralization in seeds: Developmental trends in isotopic signatures of Hackberry." *Palaeogeography, Palaeoclimatology, Palaeoecology*, vol. 138, no. 1–4, Apr. 1998, pp. 259–269, https://doi.org/10.1016/s0031-0182(97)00122-3.

Jahren, Hope. *Lab Girl*. Alfred A. Knopf, 2016.

Miller, Donald G, and Anantanarayanan Raman. "Host–plant relations of gall-inducing insects." *Annals of the Entomological Society of America*, vol. 112, no. 1, 8 Oct. 2018, pp. 1–19, https://doi.org/10.1093/aesa/say034.

Moerman, Daniel E. *Native American Medicinal Plants: An Ethnobotanical Dictionary*. Timber Press, 2009.

Nichols, John, and Earl Nyholm. *A Concise Dictionary of Minnesota Ojibwe*. University of Minnesota Press, 1995.

Perlin, John. *A Forest Journey: The Role of Trees in the Fate of Civilization*, Patagonia Books, Ventura, CA, 2023.

Reed, Leslie. "FDR's 'Great Wall of Trees' Continues to Provide Lessons." *Newsroom | University of Nebraska–Lincoln*, 2017, news.unl.edu/newsrooms/today/article/fdr-s-great-wall-of-trees-continues-to-provide-lessons.

Rupp, Rebecca. *Red Oaks & Black Birches: The Science and Lore of Trees*. Storey Communications, 1992.

Selker, Lauren. "Meadowcroft: Peering into America's Ancient Past". *Pennsylvania Center for the Book*, 2010.

Sherman, Sean, and Beth Dooley. *The Sioux Chef's Indigenous Kitchen*. University of Minnesota Press, 2017.

Smith, Welby Richmond. *Trees and Shrubs of Minnesota: The Complete Guide to Species Identification*. University of Minnesota Press, 2008.

Taylor, Fred. "Variations in Sugar Content of Maple Sap." *Agricultural Experiment Station*, University of Vermont and State Agricultural College Burlington, Bulletin 587, 1956.

Thomas, Peter A. *Trees: Their Natural History*. 2nd ed., Cambridge University Press, 2014.

Wohlleben, Peter. *The Hidden Life of Trees: What They Feel, How They Communicate: Discoveries from a Secret World*. Greystone Books, 2016.

Northern white cedar tree ID tag

Our Tree Treks

Chet Mirocha

Stephanie at white spruce. Photo by Shevek McKee.

Chet at black walnut. Photo by Julie Mirocha.

Stephanie at Ohio buckeye. Photo by Shevek McKee.

About the Author and Artist

STEPHANIE MIROCHA GREW UP CLIMBING TREES AND EXPLORING THE CITY park across from her childhood home. Her art expression not only takes form in her passion for writing but also translates into her career as a visual artist. Besides creating the art for this book, she has illustrated four children's picture books connecting children to nature. *Frog in the House* won the 2016 Giverny Award for a science picture book in English, and *My Little Book of Bald Eagles* won 1st place, Juvenile Nonfiction, in the 2010 Next Gen Indie Book Awards. She and her scientist father shared a poetic heart and love for nature, each informing and supporting the other throughout their close relationship. Graduating from the University of Minnesota with a BA in Philosophy, Stephanie followed her free spirit and embraced the unconventional life of an artist after moving to Aitkin, a small town in north central Minnesota. This is her first written book. Her art business website is *https://stephaniemirocha.com/*.